Glass Design Innovations in Architecture

Mick Eekhout

nai010 publishers

FOREWORD

The introduction of the word 'Zappi' resulted in a steppingstone to enable the architectural society to break through the borders of thinking in architectural materialization. It represents the same kind of desire as being able to walk a high wire between the former WTC towers in New York. Philippe Petit, a French high wire walker, did exactly that by (illegally) tightening a cable at 400 m height between the Twin Towers. He walked in 1978 almost during an hour between both towers. On ground level people were watching this unrealistic but graceful spectacle in utter amazement. The mental state of mr. Petit during his walk must have been the same as designing with 'Zappi'. What is 'Zappi'? Nothing more than a designing passion. A desire to conceive known or unknown materials and constructions which in architectural respect are answers on impossible demands. In 1988 I wrote in the Dutch design magazine 'Items' that: 'Zappi' is the optimal material: flexible, strong, ductile, fluent, transparent, absorbing, fire-resistant, maintenance-free, easy to process, economic, and sustainable". I introduced the word 'Zappi' in a debate on 'The cultural meaning of iron' in the Exchange of Berlage, Amsterdam in January 1992. Professor Jaap Oosterhoff and his former PhD student, professor Mick Eekhout, were challenged to describe the limits of their professional domains and to share their ambitions concerning an ideal construction material with the audience. 'Zappi' continued its public life thanks to Mick Eekhout. He arranged that 'Zappi' gradually was interpreted as the adventurous quest itself and even mentioned in his inaugural speech 'Architecture between tradition and technology, or Zappi and the challenging product mystery' in September 1992: "Vir prudens non exspectat dum alii Zappi inveniant" or "A wise man does not wait for others to invent Zappi". 'Zappi' evolved as a key motto in research during the following years in his Chair of Product Development at TU Delft. Initially the target was a transparent structural material in many forms, even bendable glass. Later it came to represent the collective term for fundamental research in building technology. This book displays an excellent overview of the search for 'Zappi'. The shown and highlighted examples are positioned in the transition between building and external space, between form and construction, between applied art and technological professional skill. In each case a new dimension seems to be materialized. One aspect overtones in all designed cases; it almost looks too light for its function. As if Petit can fall down from his rope any minute. It seems the materialization of the unbearable lightness of being.

That is the evolution of 'Zappi', which was excellently translated by Mick Eekhout so far. And the quest goes on...

Thijs Asselbergs

Professor Thijs Asselbergs
TU Delft

CONTENTS

Centro di Arte Santander
Renzo Piano

INTRODUCTION

This book has been written after 35 years of experience in designing, developing, experimenting, certifying, and producing glass structures in architecture in my Octatube company in Delft, where I was the main designer for most of the projects. My attitude is an architect's attitude of looking for new compositions, in this case not in terms of form but technical compositions. This ambition has its origin in the time I spent as a student in the offices of the late Frei Otto in Stuttgart and of Renzo Piano in Genova in 1970. Both of them are my lifelong heroes. Renzo asked me to write my first article of 60 pages for 'Zodiac' on the Olympic Games cable net roofs in 1971 [ref.1]. In 2011, we were thus able to celebrate 40 years of writing on architecture with the presentation of my book 'Tubular Structures in Architecture to him in Genova. Between 2012 and 2014, we collaborated on the design engineering of the Centro di Arte Botin in Santander.

So I spent my time designing structural systems, developing new components, and designing new material connections, mostly innovative technical solutions. This quest brought me lifelong adventures which I had never dreamt of in the beginning, the first eight years of my architectural practice in Delft. Most architects are disconnected from the actual building process. Their offices are always off-site. At Octatube I combined from the very beginning thinking and making: the architect's and engineering office was in the same place as the factory where the components were made. The engineering office is the core of the company. Steel was cut and welded, aluminium was cut and machined there. All metal components were coated in a separate coating facility, assembled and eventually shipped. More importantly, a big part of the factory is devoted to experiments, the Octatube Laboratory is used for mock-ups and test rigs where materials and performances are tested up to the level of certification.

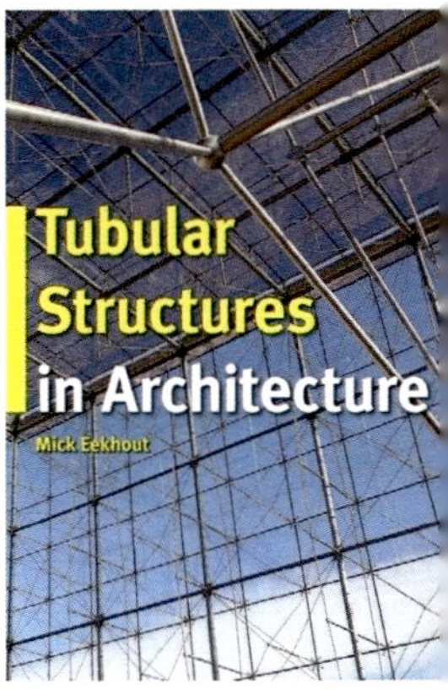

Fig. 3 Mick Eekhout, 'Tubular Structures in Architecture', 2011.

Links: Fig. 4 Architect Frei Otto (1925-1995).

Rechts: Fig. 5 Architect Renzo Piano (1937).

Opposite page: Fig.1 Renzo Piano and Mick Eekhout in discussion about the requirements for the Centro di Arte Botin in Santander. Renzo Piano expected "International quality".
Fig. 2 Mock-up sample of corner of one of the art center's volumes.

Fig. 6 Octatube's own production facility.

Fig. 7 Mick Eekhout shows the Quattro SR node for seismically resistant frameless glazing system.

So under one roof we can accommodate crazy ideas and wild dreams, through precise engineering and the production of components. This includes their certification to ensure application without any concern for the client. For many visiting architects the mock-up laboratory and production facility is a dream world, reminding them of Roald Dahl's 'Charlie in the Chocolate Factory'. My house was built directly behind the factory. Several times in any given day I walk from the office to my home through the factory and the laboratory, always wondering what can be improved. Materials and components inspire us to develop new technical compositions. Seeing and touching materials brought me many 'Eureka' moments. In my office a bicycle is suspended both as a piece of good design and art and also to show how many different elements and components are necessary to assemble a bike.

My professional career has been stimulated by two worlds: the industrial, design & build world of Octatube and the academic world of the faculty of Architecture TU Delft. This love for materials and components was fueled right at the beginning of my professorship at the TU Delft when in 1992 Thijs Asselbergs introduced the term 'Zappi' to describe a hypothetical structural material. 'Zappi' was to be a fully transparent and structurally reliable material for applications in architecture. Thijs Asselbergs, then town architect of Haarlem and now one of my colleague architecture professors at TU Delft, coined the word 'Zappi' for an ideal, new and non-existing material yet to be found. See the foreword. Ever since 1992, staff and students at the chair of Product Development have worked for extended periods of time on the evolution of 'Zappi' in the academic world. On the academic side the university was challenged to close this gap by developing new technologies, methods and approaches to realize this extreme material challenge.

In the industrial world of Octatube, a range of experimental glass structures has been developed in the last three decades. More practical material research on glass was undertaken by the structural engineers and the detail connections between glass and steel components were investigated, like glued glass / Quattro connections. Also new structural overall designs were developed, like post-stressed tensile stabilisations, leading to practical glass innovations, in an incremental approach, from project to project.

Two decades ago 'Free Form Designs', 'Liquid Designs' or 'Blob Designs', extensively covered by international architectural magazines, evolved and created turmoil in the building industry. They also brought challenging projects for Octatube. The 1990s gap between architects with new digital skills and refined 3D-computer programmes on the one hand and the building industry with its traditional orthogonal building systems and material processing on the other hand was widened initially. The ambitions of architects were naively high because of lack of experience. The first projects were failures. Designs were aborted and not realized. Other project designs caused almost bankruptcy of competitors of Octatube. Octatube had to solve 3D geometrical problems between components on project base. Only after a decade of experiments derived from architectural designs realistic engineering emerged, slowly. The building industry saw these designs chiefly as a nightmare more than anything else. The geometry of the new components was non-rectilinear and not flat, always curvilinear in fact. Manufacturers did not have any experience in making 3D curved panels, neither as loadbearing structures nor as cladding constructions. It seemed wise to start a transfer of technology from the nautical and aeronautical engineering industries, where fluid forms have always been very in use. At Octatube the engineering designers concluded that transfer of technology alone was not enough. Architecture appeared to be a special domain with specific characteristics, such as the large dimensions and a relatively large freedom in design, for instance Free Form Design. After the transfer of technology further adaptation of technology was necessary to achieve technical progress for applications in architecture. The large components like an aero plane hull or a ship hull can be transported separately over water, but cladding components of buildings are often larger than ships. The cannot be transported in large dimensions by road transport and have to be assembled from smaller elements. The topic of Free Form Technology was explored further in a publication 'Free Form Technology from Delft' [ref.2, fig.8] Examples of large sized components are the large glass fibre reinforced polyester wings of the Rabin Center in Tel Aviv up to a size of 20x30m2 roof surface without any visible seams. This project was documented in a book published in 2016 'Lord of the Wings' [ref 3, fig. 9].

Fig. 8 Mick Eekhout, 'Free Form Technology Delft', 2016 [ref. 2]

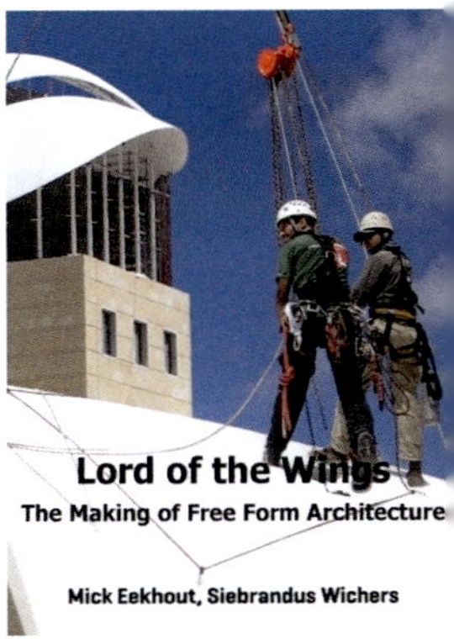

Fig. 9 Mick Eekhout, Siep Wychers , 'Lord of the Wings', 2016 [ref. 3]

Fig. 10 Exterior of the Rabin Center, Tel Aviv, 2006, architect Moshe Safdie.

Fig. 11 Interior of the Rabin Center, Tel Aviv.

In the last three decades the quest for innovative glass technology has triggered a careful and incremental research and development process. This was partly based on dreams, wild ideas, bold designs, ingenious innovations, entrepreneurship, building projects and supportive clients on the industrial side. On the academic side it was based on wider contemplations, philosophy, more theoretical research and long-term development work and methodological thinking at the university. Practice inspires theory which, in turn, lays the foundations for further inventions and innovations in the industry. The two worlds of academia on the one hand and the building industry on the other were thus closely connected in order to boost inventions, innovations, mock-ups, experimental zero series and even real building projects. Such a collaboration between industry and academic research, a process of mutual stimulation, can lead to a complete new vocabulary in building technology.

This dual incremental development is partly due to the small business character (SME – Small and Medium Entreprises) of the building industry and needs to be fed by a constant flow of projects with their typical deadlines.

This book contains a mixture of realized short-term design and development Octatube projects and longer term research and development projects undertaken in the Chair of Product Development in Architecture at TU Delft.

Opposite page: Fig. 12 The construction of the glass fibre-reinforced polyester sandwich wings for the Rabin Center in Tel Aviv required the work of abseilers 40 m above the ground. Experiments do not allow fear of height.

עבודות
הנדסת

Fig. 13 Cold-bent laminated glass panels at a pavilion at the horticultural exposition Floriade, Haarlemmermeer, 2002, Asymptote Architects, New York .

Together, they provide a picture of the very personal research, development and design quest for architectural glass innovations. Without the devoted crews of Octatube and staff and students of the Chair these results would not have been possible, of course.

In 1991, entering the academic world seemed attractive to me. At Octatube, worldwide adventures beckoned but there was hardly an intellectual debate. Now, after some 30 years as a full professor at TU Delft, I can better appreciate the wider scope and 'can do' mentality of an international private company compared to that of a university research group. Architects are typically also concerned with societal needs, beyond their immediate building tasks. While clients normally do not reward this concern, it serves to advance the profession. Architects are beta-engineers, but also aware of alpha and gamma aspects in societies before their designs are applied and accepted as successful. Alpha important for the users and gamma for the money, legal side and building permissions.

In 1982, we started Octatube since no contractor was prepared to realize the innovative designs with architectural glass we had developed previously at our architectural office. That marked the beginning of my personal transition from a mere architect to an inventor and builder. I never regretted this move, although building technology doesn't entail the glamour that surrounds architecture. By now, the achievements of three decades of innovative glass design are substantial and worthwhile documenting. While designing the technical side of architecture the invention and innovation govern. And, again, these achievements were only made possible by the collective effort of the collaborators at Octatube and of the staff members at TU Delft.

Professor Zygmunt Makowski (1922–2005), the world expert on space structures at the time and dean of the civil engineering faculty of Surrey university, said to the young student Eekhout, in his 4th study year at the time (1972) and working on a roof design for Feyenoord soccer stadium in Rotterdam: "*Mr. Eekhout, please never go into research, always remain a designer.*" In 2002, he was still was so impressed with the projects of his former student that he awarded him the prestigious 'Pioneers' Award in Spatial Structures' of the University of Surrey. The joy of designing is always there. Design can surprise and astonish, can provide a solution for a complicated problem. Research is used to chart unknown territories. Research guides one on a path of discoveries with short and big steps. But when it comes to solutions, the force of design is favoured above the process of research. Therefore, a strong design component in academic research is an efficient tool. This approach, called 'Research by Design', uses a disciplinary methodology developed over my long career as a design professional. In this book a short explanation of the virtues of design development methodology is given, which is further described in my book 'Methodology for Product Development in Architecture', 2008, [ref 4].

Fig. 14 The glass water basin at the Floriade, Haarlemmermeer, 2002, had to accommodate the extremely heavy load of 1400 kg/m2. Asymptote Architects.

Fig. 15 Mick Eekhout's book 'Bridging the gap', 2009, described a master plan for Dutch university research for the building sector in crisis.

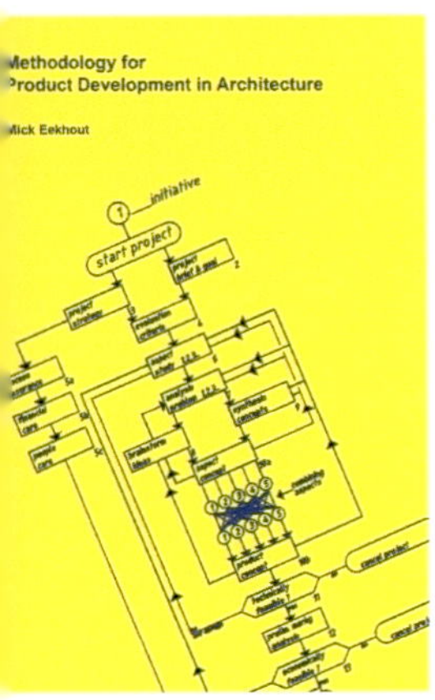

Middle: Fig. 16 '3TU Speerpunt Bouw Leerstoelenboek', 2009, a publication on the joint forces of 80 Dutch professors in the built environment in order to jump over the then recession.

Bottom: Fig. 17 Mick Eekhout, 'Methodology for Product Development in Architecture', 2008.

Some of the design dreams came true through lifelong engineering, producing and building, while others yet have to become reality. It has always been my dream to leave on earth footprints in the form of realized designs. Part of this dream is to lead a group of enthusiastic young people at Octatube, at Delft Design, at Booosting, at the Chair of Product Development and at the group of 3TU. Building Research. Another part of it is to contemplate and write about creative designs, to combine academic and practical work to boost innovations which have a positive effect on the future of society.

Another initiative was a national research and development programme 'Bridging the Gap', [ref.5] for the Dutch building industry started in 2009 in order to jump over the building recession. This master programme was to take the supply and demand of both the academic and the industrial side of the building sector into account. The 2009 publication '3TU Speerpunt Bouw Leerstoelenboek' [ref. 6] summarized statements by. 80 professors from what is called 3TU, the three Dutch technical universities Delft, Eindhoven and Enschede, related to the building industry. The Netherlands are small enough, and with only three technical universities most of the professors in the building faculties know each other, so this overview was easy to achieve. For the time being, the master programme has been shelved, as the deans lost control to a new national research institution, which they did not favour.

The dualism between designing and building, between thinking and doing in my case is rooted in the father-son-relationship of Jan Eekhout who was a building contractor and his eldest son Mick who became an architect. At Octatube, we started out with making structures by hand for artists like Krijn Giezen and Loes van der Horst. Already in 1975 the first design & build project was the artwork 'Bijlmobiel' in Amsterdam. Later the model laboratory became a small workshop. And the small workshop became a prototype factory. A few years later a complete factory was organized, paving the way for the extraordinary designs (such as stretched membranes, space frames and glass structures) the firm is known for. The design office became a medium-size design & build company of 100 fte staff, working all over the whole world. The design & build approach facilitated taking up wild ideas from the design stage and develop them further, have them certified and eventually built as prototypes in projects. And these design concepts were then applied in zero series for many lightweight constructions and structures for roofs and façades in architecture.

Fellow architects would come and be treated to a quick development of their design ideas in a conducive thinking-and-doing environment. Many architects almost saw Octatube as their own laboratory during a collaborative project.

In this way, our approach was similar to Renzo Piano Building Workshop where designing, developing and engineering of new constructions in new materials lead to prototyping. The real manufacturing and building takes the process and the responsibility and liability one step further.

This book has been written to give an overview of the glass designs that originate from the design & build company Octatube and the research results from staff and students of the Chair of Product Development, both led by Mick Eekhout as the director and the professor. The combination of the two worlds enabled developments that would have been impossible otherwise.

Essentially it was the design & build approach that resulted in a whole range of technical innovations. Starting with the first self-built artworks with Loes van der Horst and Krijn Giezen in the 1970s and 1980s and followed by the establishment of Octatube as a company in 1983, the firm now looks back on a long history of continuous technical developments. This also comprises unusual tasks like the glass fibre-reinforced composite shell wings of the Rabin Center in Tel Aviv with Moshe Safdie and the 30 m cardboard dome with Shigeru Ban in Amsterdam. It led in 1995 to the installation of the Prototype Laboratory of the Chair of Product Development in Architecture at TU Delft, where more than 1500 students engineered, produced and built a material prototype according to their own design in 25 years [ref.7]

The hands-on approach at Octatube Prototype Laboratory proved to be very stimulating, for example in the cases of glued glass connections and cold twisted glass. Both innovations had their origin in the use of materials that happened to be available in the factory after a brain wave. Glued glass instead of holes in the glass and a glass industry refusing guarantees and cold twisting happened on a project to make a more economical solution.

Fig. 18 Bijlmobiel, Amsterdam designed and built with Loes van der Horst (1975), one of the very first design&build projects.

Fig. 19 Artwork designed and built with Krijn Giezen, Maritime Museum Amsterdam (1985).

Octatube engineers, further developed and engineered, fully tested and certified and eventually brought into practice and then repeated many times. For cold twisting of glass the concept was only fully understood after the first project had been completed. The theory was developed after the practice had proven itself. Once the projects with their newly developed technologies had been published, other companies applied similar principles, so the innovations were spread and then widely accepted in the building industry.

Fig. 20 Mick Eekhout recognizes at the Renzo Piano Building Workshop his hero Renzo Piano as the carpenter's son.

Fig. 21 Student work: Experiment with an all cardboard dome with carboard nodes at the TU Prototype Laboratory.

Fig 22 Student work: close-up of a Chinese fan to be used as a sunscreen in front of a circular glass plane.

ABOUT THIS BOOK:

The first chapter deals with the relationship between design, development and research. It explains the methodology often used in either discipline. It looks at the position of the glass structure designer both active in the industry and in academia, to show how both worlds inspire each other.

The second chapter is written on the topic of the structural use of glass, the making of prototypes and the advantages of a design & build approach in a resourceful company. It is dealing with Octatube's remarkable projects of the last three decades that manipulated glass as a structural material: under bending, compression, tension and combinations of these forces.

The third chapter displays the different connection methods, nodal systems for frameless glazing, from the conventional mechanical fixings via the half-mechanical/half-chemical connections to the fully glued connections.

The fourth chapter is on the quest for 'Zappi', an ambition almost beyond the horizon, a moonshot. A term coined in 1992 that describes the quest for a theoretical material with omnipotent qualities.

The fifth chapter is on super slender steel structures and the development these systems took. From the 52 m high suspended façade of the OZ building in Tel Aviv to the 14 m high cable-stayed structures of INHolland in Delft where the cables are running through the interspace of the double glass panels and the 40 m span cable net glass facades of the Market Hall in Rotterdam.

The sixth chapter deals with the 'Free Form Technology' research results of master students and PhD students and applications in practical projects by Octatube. The cold twisting of glass is an outcome of such a synergy between industry and university research. It describes extremes of hot and cold bending, low temperatures and the inspiration building design owes to yacht design.

The seventh chapter is on glass fins, back to the roots of structural behaviour and safety for the building users under these roofs. The chapter gives a conclusion of the virtues of the approach of 'designing and building' or 'design & build' and provides an outlook for the adventures still ahead of us: the glass footprint.
The products shown in this chapter are steps forward in this quest. The '50% Zappi Glass' research proposal was written with an eye on the development of glass façades with only 50% of the embedded energy of the current glass facades and energy-neutral maintenance to be reached within the coming decade. The entire glass sector has to contribute in collaboration towards that goal.

CHAPTER 1.
CONDITIONS FOR GLASS DESIGN INNOVATIONS

The designer's portfolio and the professor's activities originate from the point of view of technical design with a creative and spontaneous start and a systematic and methodological process approach. To design and develop new concepts means to undertake experiments before these concepts can be realized. Other parties in the building team do not bother about this innovative ambition of the designer. So the designer has to show that new concepts are trustworthy and by leading a methodical process without essential steps left out.

DESIGN & BUILD APPROACH

This creative approach has led to processes of implementing new designs. In a design & build firm, the designer / company director is not only responsible for the design ideas, concepts and engineering, but also for the production of components and the assembly of the total technical artefact. This combination of design & build functions relieves other parties who, in a technical sense, are not as capable as the engineers. Thus the engineers enjoy extended opportunities, but at the same time have to assume broader responsibilities and also liabilities. In Germany this is not a frequently used practice in the building industry and it complicates the legal work. German contractors typically do not want to assume responsibility for the design. 'Design & build' does not have a proper definition in the EU norms. It has the potential to create many discussions before, during and after the process.

Although this design & build approach practiced at Octatube has remained rare in Western-European countries, it has certainly proven to be fruitful in respect to innovations. The design & build process is an integral part of Octatube's success.

EXPERIMENTAL PROTOTYPE LABORATORY

The design & build method has also been used also in the Prototype Lab of the Chair of Product Development at TU Delft since 1995, which was established 3 years after the start of the Chair. The influence from practice to students led them to work methodologically, which they normally were not used to do. It also evoked discussions on methodology with other scientists on the university, for example with town planners, machine engineers and industrial designers. For myself working both on the creative but also on the methodological level resulted in many innovations. I am most fortunate as a designer to have a private laboratory cum production factory where new designs can be developed and experiments can be conducted. At the end almost all of the inventive and innovative designs have been realized in practice. By publishing on the results as a professor I always have regarded my private laboratory also to be my offshored experimental academic laboratory.

Opposite page: Fig. 23 Exterior of the glass cube for Santander Bank, Madrid, Alphonso Millanes, 2008.

CHAPTER 1.1
Design, Development and Research

During discussions on TU between designing and engineering colleagues we found that in spite of differences, the common goals and identities between different designers, developers and researchers was easy to clarify. The scheme of figure 24 was proposed for that purpose. It displayed the connections between the two extreme poles of Fundamental Research on the extreme left side and Artistic Design on the extreme right side. The intermediate domains of Fundamental Technical Research, System Development, Product Development and Technical Application Design have a mutual relationship with their neighbouring domains of fundamental research on the one hand and application one the other. Each domain has its own laws, set of rules, habits and players. Yet they are very much linked by these fundamental or applied relationships. It displays the position of designers in a technical world of researchers and developers. The left neighbor looks to its right neighbor for application knowhow, but the same neighbor looks to the left for more fundamental knowhow.

DESIGN AND SCIENCE

Most of current architecture is in fact not much of a science, but rather an engineering achievement. One has to admit that most of the contemporary architecture does not have the capital 'A' of 'Architecture', but is the result of architectural engineering. In the eyes of scientists, architecture does not qualify as a science. Similarly, most of civil engineering is engineering after all and not much of a science either. But both are necessary in society for applications.

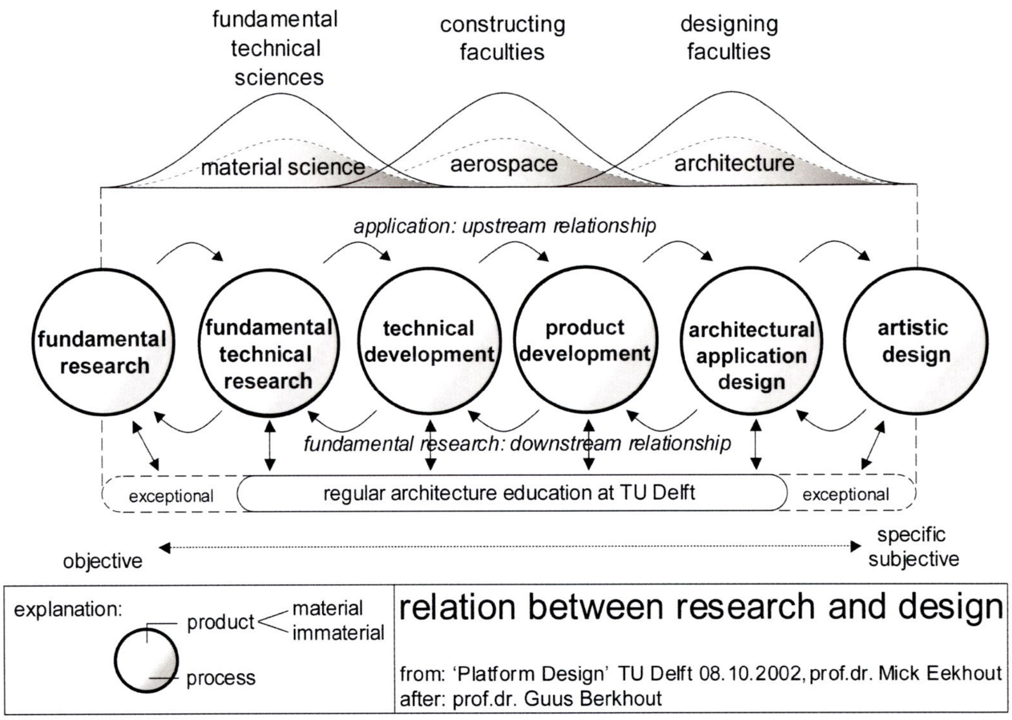

Fig. 24 Relationship between Research, Development and Design

A great part of the work of a Dutch building designer is engineering. Only a small part of the daily activities can be called science, design science or engineering science. Mainly new and experimental architecture needs science in order to be developed and to come to fruition. Vice versa, only a small number of projects is interesting in a scientific way. In this book, technical designs are conceived for applications in architecture. There is ample experimental architectural design that deserves to be called 'scientific design', bringing together 'Technical Application Design' from the adjacent figure with 'Fundamental Technical Research', whenever necessary. If one loses the fear of the unknown, excursions from one's own domain to other domains can be undertaken to obtain new knowledge and insight. 'Zappi' was an excursion from the domains of 'Product Development' and 'Technical Application Design' into 'Fundamental Research'. Zappi was researched in the Chair of Product Development by Dr. Fred Veer between 1995 and 2005, mainly through the dissertations of graduation students. The impossible goal of chemical and mechanical characteristics of Zappi glass as stated in 1992 [i.e. unbreakable transparant ductile and strong structural material] was not found. This did not mean that the Zappi excursion was a failure. Many incremental steps forward were set in the development of fail-safe glass. The end result was a triple laminated glass beam where the lamination provided the ductility. In Chapter 7.6, figure 300 the end result of the Zappi quest in the Octatube company is displayed in the form of an overhead triple laminated glass beam which was fully broken and kept in place for four weeks. Although the glass beam was sagging under the applied deadweight, it did not collapse.

SCIENCE IN DESIGN AT TU DELFT

At a University of Technology many scientists from different faculties have complementary knowledge and sometimes opposite opinions, which makes excursions into the world of science worthwhile for architects.

Chemical scientists look as much to architecture for applications of their findings than architects look to chemistry for more fundamental inspiration. The interest is mutual. This has resulted at TU Delft in the formation of a design platform for professors and staff members interested in design from most of the faculties: architecture, industrial design, civil engineering, marine engineering, material engineering, aeronautics. In meetings design was debated and differences and similarities were defined. As part of this design platform, I was able to organize two 'Delft Science in Design' congresses in 2005 and 2007.

In the realm of architecture itself, there is also a difference between fundamental and applied knowledge. Architecture has a theoretical base, an engineering or technological core and comprises applied design. It is the task of university faculties to enable fundamental research in the

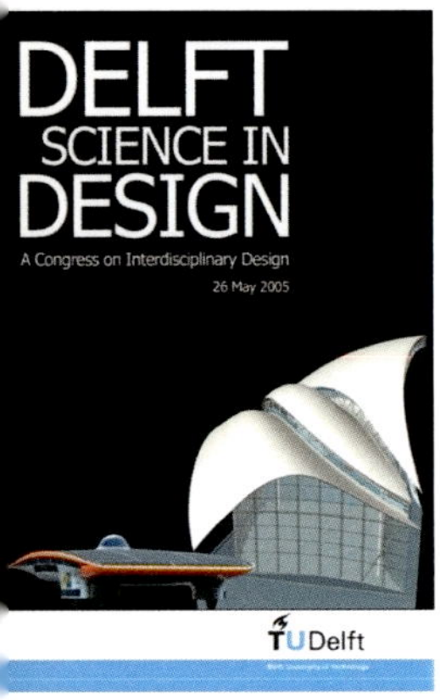

Fig. 25 Delft Science in Design, 2005.

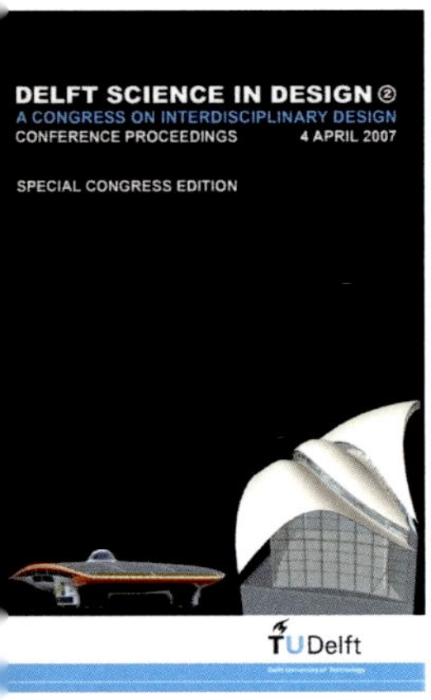

Fig. 26 Delft Science in Design, 2007.

various disciplines, both in design, in engineering as well and in development.

Typically, schools of architecture focus on fundamental research yet with an eye on practical design applications. The actual designing and engineering of projects, however, is done in architectural offices. It is no wonder therefore that 90% of the professors of the faculty of architecture at TU Delft are part-timers, with one foot in academia and the other foot in the design or engineering world or in the industry. At Delft only 5 out of 40 full professors in architecture are full-time, all 35 others only part-time.

The disdain of fundamental scientists towards application-directed architecture is unfounded, in particular since applications contribute to introducing fundamental research to society at large. I use to say to my fellow professors from science; "Architecture is like a tunnel, funneling the results of science to society". For a designer even writing a book is perceived as an act of design. Writing is designing with words and meanings. The contents of this book originate from design concepts in collaboration with clients (usually project architects from around the world), with whom I had the privilege to collaborate on redesigning or improving the detailing of their concepts. As such this book is a proof of the force of design through a period of three decades in glass developments.

CHAPTER 1.2

The Art of Product Development

THREE BASIC TYPES OF BUILDING PRODUCTS

Product development recognizes three main types of products: standard products, system products and special products.

Product design and development for standard building products is usually done within the producing industry, sometimes with the aid of industrial product designers or architectural technicians. The absence of clients necessitates sufficient marketing activities during the development processes.

System building products are designed and developed on two levels: on the first 'system' level as a general system product solving principle problems and on the second 'application' level after the product has been sold for a specific application in a building project. In the second phase the project architect plays a role, since further design and engineering work is directed towards fitting in the specific overall design in an architectural project.

Special building products or special components are designed by the project architect, developed and engineered by the product industry in collaboration with the project architect and produced after that phase. A good dialogue between project architect and the manufacturer is essential to ensure good quality.

This book documents special building components and system products, evolved from initially experimental designs of special components after a process of adaptation and integration of practical experience. Industrialized space frame designs are typical examples of system designs. Quite differently, free-form glass design experiments lead to inventions, experimental applications and innovations and thus create refinements and improvements for a range of special free-form components, which are also called special products. Material, sizes and production methods are often new. That is the conclusion of the first decade of Free Form Technology. Only in the second and last decade Free Form Technology became mature.

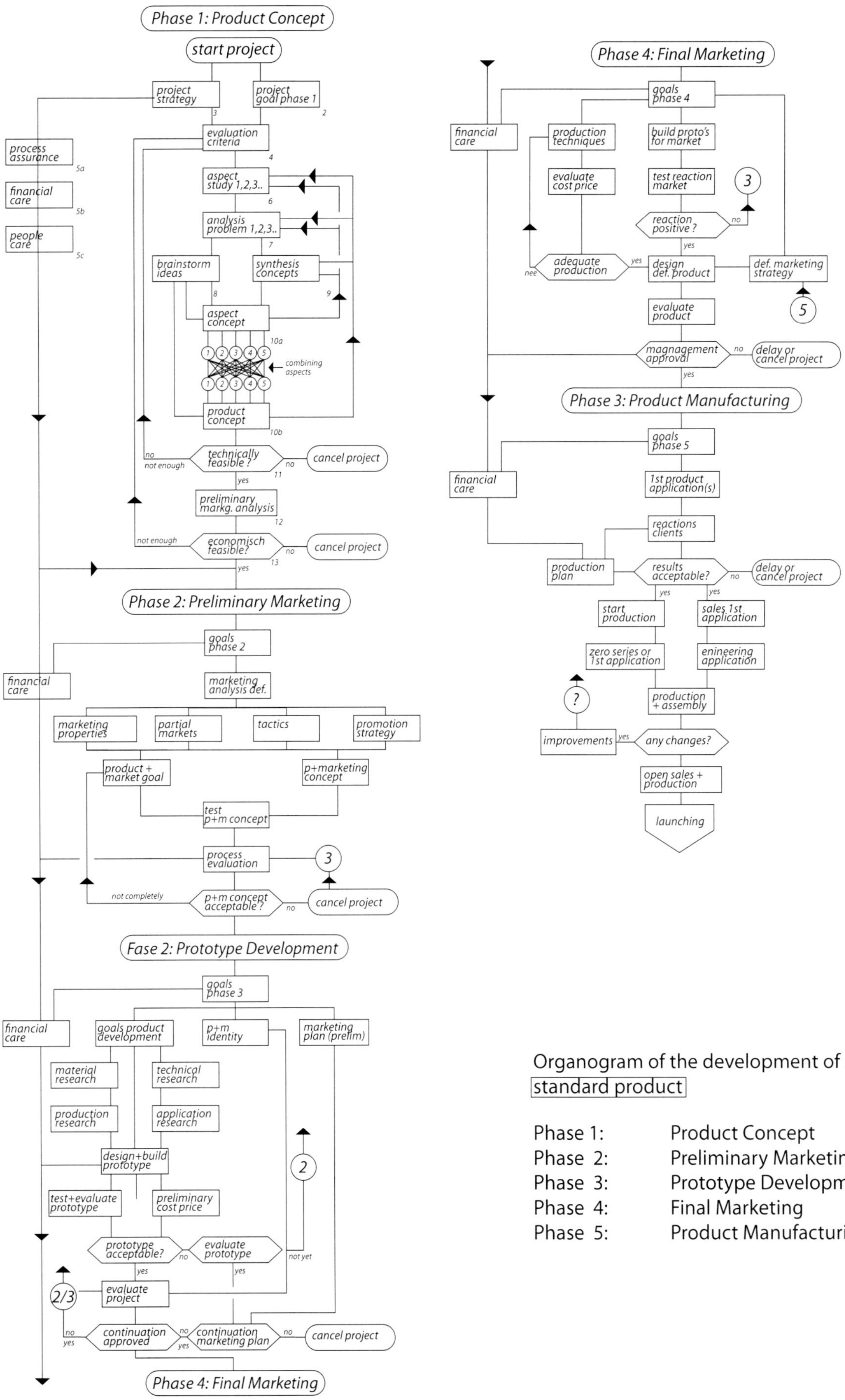

Organogram of the development of a standard product

Phase 1:	Product Concept
Phase 2:	Preliminary Marketing
Phase 3:	Prototype Development
Phase 4:	Final Marketing
Phase 5:	Product Manufacturing

ORGANOGRAM FOR DEVELOPMENT OF NEW PRODUCTS

The Organogram (Fig. 27) illustrates a methodological approach for product development and links design via methodology to science. This methodology is explained in my book Methodology in Product Development in Architecture, 2008, [ref. 10]. The different steps are explained in that book after giving a theoretical background on standard building products, building systems / system products and special products or special components for buildings. In case of the organogram of standard products (Fig. 26), the development process is divided into five main stages:

- Concept design
- Preliminary marketing
- Prototype development
- Definitive marketing
- Product manufacturing

The different steps or activities are positioned subsequently, respectively parallel to one another, much depending on the very activities on the desired building product. These schemes are the general master plans of any development process. Students who have problems with prefabricated texts and theories often are told that they have to follow the Wittgenstein's proposition 4.65 from his Tractatus from 1923, [ref. 11], where he states that one better follows the given theories above them before one leaves them and throws them away as one's own specific insight fits better.

A methodological approach to problems or challenges prevents the designer from drowning in complexity or chaos. It can also bring a better solution than the original first conceptual thought. For more information reference is given to the forementioned Methodology for Product Development in Architecture. A methodology is given for standard building products which are industrially produced, for building systems which need additional information before prefabrication is done and for special building components which are designed by architects for special project buildings. The full organogram (Fig. 27) illustrates the flow of activities for standard products. Special components have a much shorter organogram without the two marketing phases since the client is already known. This is explained in Fig. 29.

SPECIAL BUILDING COMPONENTS

Special components are technical parts of buildings that have to be designed and developed specifically as there are no standard or system solutions on the market. Typically, the architect specifies both the form and the material of this customized component. In the following section an example is given.

Opposite page: Fig. 27
Organogram of the development of standard products in 5 phases.

Figs. 28 Proposal for glass columns in the Berlage room of the Faculty of Architecture TU Delft to improve for everyone sitting at the back of the room the view towards the lecturn.

GLASS COLUMNS FOR THE BERLAGE ROOM

A glass column in a large room can serve to guide structural forces from the superstructure to the substructure below floor level while not creating a massive obtrusive presence in the space. The example are the two glass columns proposed for the socalled 'Berlage' room of the Architecture faculty of TU Delft. In the current building of the faculty of Architecture, built in the 1920s the space is quite governed by two concrete columns. The existing columns are disastrous for the visual experience of the room while glass columns would be far less obtrusive. This proposal was presented in my farewell lecture as a professor in 2015 [ref.12], but unlike one might suppose in a well-known school of architecture, there has been no serious initiative so far to remove these visually very disturbing concrete columns and to substitute them by glass columns. This is an architectural design concept.

In the *first phase* of finding the design concept the important evaluation criteria are structural liability, invulnerability to mechanical damages, transparency and flush detailing. The study aspects are compression forces, buckling forces, glass materials, glass connections, head/foot details, resulting transparency and installation procedure. Each of these aspects has to be analyzed individually and the best solution for each requirement has to be established. These solutions are combined and the result could be a component concept, in this case the concept for a glass column.

The next step is to consider whether the concept is technically feasible, with an unknown experimental phase ahead. If not, the project is stopped. After the technical feasibility study the economical feasibility is investigated. In this phase, the project can also be stopped because of lack of funding.

The *second phase* of prototype development has as its core the technical development in the following four areas: material research (glass tubes and flat plates, buckling tests, glued connections), technical research (two glass tubes fed into each other and laminated, laminated flat glass ribs, glued connections of metals), production research (glue technology, flatness, tolerances, protection in boxes) and application research (structural analysis of compression forces in current concrete columns and proposed glass columns with upper and lower hinges and installation of glass columns with foot and head detail, post-stressing and measuring of actual stresses). Singular and integrated structural tests may be necessary as to the behaviour of glass tubes and glass plates. Possibly the result will be that the commercial circular glass tubes do not suffice, but a customized component has to be assembled of three laminated glass ribs in triangular connection, with metal connectors (piano hinges) and stainless steel top and bottom foot details. The preliminary cost price is estimated.

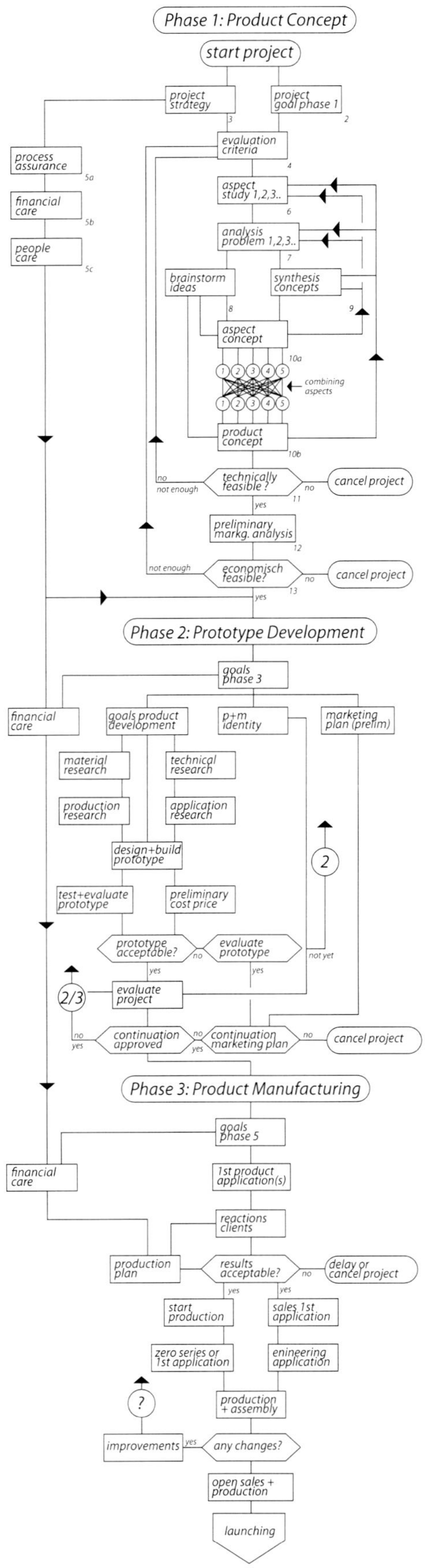

Fig. 29 Organogram of the development of special building components in only three phases.

It is determined whether a proposal is technically, aesthetically and financially acceptable. If the structural analysis is adequate, further research testing and more analysis may be required, up until the final structural analysis report is finished. If need be, in case of a very experimental design, a third party may be invited to act as a second opinion professional engineer, like in Germany a 'Zulassungsingenieur'. At that point the outcome of the different evaluations can still cause the project to be abandoned. But after approval the project can go on into the next phase.

The *third phase* of product manufacturing starts with the conventional prudent considerations of a production and installation plan. It is important to find a commercial production company willing to undertake this production with the necessary quality and responsibility. The resulting price has to incorporate the sub-productions, the assembly, the installation and the liability for this sensitive building component after installation. The glass production involves various steps: the thermally pre-stressed glass rib panels, accurately grinded and polished, the lamination process and the glueing process of the stainless steel elements to the glass, including the preparatory work of glass grinding for optimal glue adhesion. The glass assembly will take place in a laboratory-like workshop environment. The foot and head details and plates will be glued and connected, the total assembly will be tested in a test rig up to a certain maximum load as required in the analysis report. At the building site the two concrete columns have been cut off and temporarily replaced by steel suoorts with a space in between them for finally positioning the glass column. The columns are transported to the site and installed between the lower and upper column ends already in place, consisting of a stainless steel plate exactly positioned in height. After sliding the columns between upper and lower plates the temporary supports are released and the glass columns are loaded. The forces are then measured and compared with the theoretical stresses. For the reason of vulnerability it would be wise to integrate stress gauges to measure the stresses in the glass columns.

Finally, the evaluation of the project after completion will indicate whether these glass columns can be applied in other projects as well. In that case, the originally customized product becomes a system with different applications for different projects while maintaining the product essence. The making of the glass columns is here taken as an example of a careful methodical approach for special components or special products.

CHAPTER 1.3

An External Laboratory for Academia?

For architects practical design has a higher attraction than education. The thrill of the design adventure gets lost in the repetition of teaching. An architect loves to design and education is an extra. That is why full-time architectural professors without an office are scarce in the Netherlands. In contrast with the few full-time professors of architecture (5 out of 40 professors at the architecture faculty of TU Delft) the part-time professor usually has a design practice as an architect or an engineer. He stands with one foot in the building industry, with the other in the academic world. For the students this offers the chance to hear lectures and receive supervision from the best and most up-to-date professionals. Part-time professors usually conduct not much of the research at the university themselves.

OFF-SHORED DESIGN OFFICES FOR ACADEMIA

My proposition here is to integrate innovations developed within the professors' private practice into their laboratory work at the university and to then elevate these innovations by means of scientification. Professors could analyze the processes and products in a scientific way, publish, debate and discuss these results so that their design, development and research work becomes part of the academic world of science. In this vein, I consider the best Octatube projects also as a contribution towards my academic research & development work. This book is to document the achievements in this realm.

Fig. 30 Mick Eekhout at the presentation of his eight new books one year after his farewell lecture as a full professor in 2016.

In each design office there is also ample engineering to be done. At Octatube we have established the rule that up to 20% of the contracts have to be innovative and experimental. About these projects articles and books are written. Lectures are given and debates are provoked. It is the modus operandi of a part-time full-professor who makes a contribution to the world of science, which usually is taken up by other academics. In a design company, academic debates are scarce. Debates and discussions between professionals and architectural academics happen mainly during and after lectures, symposia and conferences.

My whole professional life has been devoted to designing with a scientific interest and to developing a generation of glass inventions and innovations now applied worldwide. Research provided the knowledge and insights necessary to make excellent designs. So the designer of objects (buildings and prominent part of buildings) and of systems (later to be applied in building projects) should be characterized by a continuous interest in new things, in inventions and certainly innovations.

Fig. 31 Technical glass innovation by Octatube as a highly post-stressed cable net structure for two glass facades for the well-known Markthal in Rotterdam, MVRDV, 2014.

Construction needs have always been fulfilled with contemporary technical means. Industrially produced float glass has been in use since Pilkington invented the float glass process in 1959. For 60 years glass panes have been enriched industrially to perform ever better. One of the most important primary building materials, reinforced concrete, is already 100 years old and mature as a construction material. It has lost its material expression. There is little interest to innovate in concrete. Generally speaking, research in established materials like reinforced concrete but also glass suffers from the economical 'Law of Diminishing Returns'. In other words, one has to invest ever more energy to produce ever smaller gains.

Looking to my students I see that many young architects think they can conquer the world by their designs comprising their own selections and innovations of materials. They have to change fashion from the previous generation. They have a particular interest in new materials and new techniques, often developed by technology transfer. Disciplines such as nautical and aeronautical engineering play a role here. When working with glass, practical impulses from the building industry are valuable. Often the tenders for challenging projects are useful where specialists on glass structures are asked for an innovative contribution.

The structural use of glass has been one of the most interesting items of scientific technical design in architecture in the past 30 years, sparking substantial design, research and development efforts. It started in my company in designing the Glass Music Hall in Amsterdam, Pieter Zaanen, 1990. After my inauguration at the TU Delft, this quest for unknown potentialities was referred after 1992 to as 'the quest for Zappi'. In line with our marketing-influenced times 'Zappi' had a name before it had any design properties and a firm material identity. The marketing worked so well that only one year after publication of the inaugural lecture Architecture between Tradition and Experimentation, in 1993, Asahi Glass Company from Japan sent scouts to find out more about the progress of Zappi. At the time, Asahi had a staff of 200 working in their laboratories and at TU Delft only a handful of people were working on the project.

The quest for Zappi was a bit later strongly linked to the emerging Free-form technology the end of the 1990s. It led to special Blob building components with specific 3D-forms. These designs are directly related to the new 3D design programmes used by a group of avant-garde free-form architects and designers. They originate from the introduction and use of computer presentation and design programmes like Maya, Rhino, 3D Studio Max and so on. Within a few hours a skilled computer designer can generate such complex building forms that the collective technical engineers of the building team have years of work. Understandably these 3D-programmes widen the gap between the ambitions and wishes of the architect on the one hand and the capacities of the largely 2D-producing building industry on the other hand. Only a few companies have dared to step into this vacuum. The growing gap between these 3D design programmes and the conventional mechanical engineering programmes in use in certified production technologies has to be bridged by new Free-form technology.

At Octatube the quest for Zappi started already in 1988 with the graduation work of civil engineering student Rik Grashoff (see fig. 70).

Fig. 32 Cover of publication of the inaugural speech by Dr. Mick Eekhout, Architecture between Tradition and Experimentation, 1992 [ref.13].

Fig. 33 The Octatube production factory in Delft. .

Because of the limited resources at both Octatube and at TU Delft, the only approach to be followed in both working environments was typically the incremental approach. Renzo Piano referred to this as 'a step-by-step approach'. Over the years this incremental approach has shown to produce a slow, but continuous process, stepped up by three basic characteristics in the Octatube company:

1. Continuous development of innovative building products and systems;
2. Synergy of architectural, structural and industrial design;
3. Integration of designing & engineering and production & realization.

The practical design & development projects and issues of Octatube are usually short-term directed. Avant-garde technical architects in the Netherlands usually are the first to pick up a tendency in design and to prepare the material solutions for it. This was the case in space frames in the late 1970s and frameless glazing in the late 1980s.

Fig. 34 Mock-up of segment of the cold warped glass panels on long triple layered glass fins roof for the Victoria & Albert Museum, London, architect Muma, engineer Tim Macfarlane, 2009.

Fig. 35 Segment prototype of the INHolland cable façade with pre-stressed cables through the inter-space between the both glass panes of the double glass panels, architect Rijk Rietveld, 2009.

CHAPTER 1.4
Prototype Laboratory for Students

Three years after my inauguration at the Chair of Product Development a workshop and laboratory for students was started in 1995 and established in the education programme. This workshop was called the Prototype Laboratory, a hands-on prototype workshop whose concept was to some extent inspired by Renzo Piano's Building Workshop. The design & build method of Octatube was adopted: students had to take care of the project from the conceptual phase up to the completion phase, a true design & build process. This laboratory combined the fields of design and engineering with production and building. In practice it would bring together the abilities of architects and engineers with those of the producing and building industry. The main objective was that students should lose their fear of materials. And those practical experiences in producing and assembling broadened the horizon of these future designers. Practical knowledge is particularly useful for experimental projects and for optimizing of initial designs.

Generally speaking, students of architecture are not exposed to building practice as practical work is not obligatory in the current educational programme at TU Delft. So the design & build approach became the base of an educational Design, Engineer, Produce & Install study module. This module is currently conducted during the first semester of the fourth year, the beginning of the two-year Master of Science course after three years of the Bachelor programme. It is the first time that students have to work with their hands with real materials. They get lessons in the machining of metal, welding, bending et cetera, they learn how to work with aluminium, steel and the various types of glass, for instance float glass, fully tempered or heat-strengthened glass. The students work in groups and develop a design for a façade system. A mock-up version of this system is then produced and eventually several prototypes.

Figs. 36, 37 Results of student work at the Prototype Laboratory.

Fig. 38 Cover of The Delft Prototype Laboratory, 2016 [ref.7].

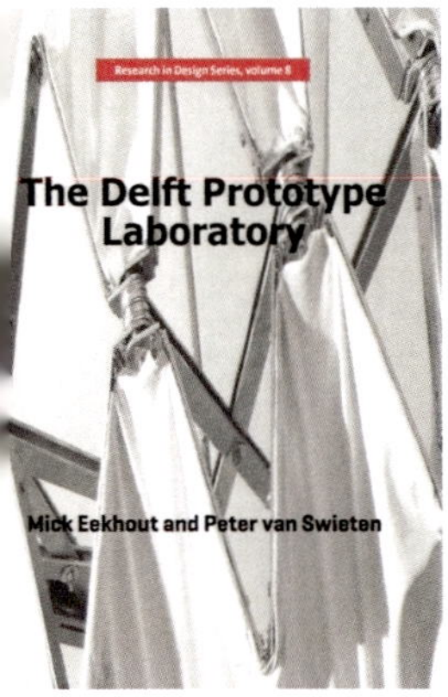

It is in this study module that students are confronted for the first time with 'tolerances'. This is the reason why the running belt was developed by Henry Ford in 1905: when the elements fit together, and this can only be done when the tolerances are always minus (smaller), they can be assembled together to form larger components without much effort.

Before that in the car ateliers around the turn of the century elements were machined off in case they were too big to be assembled. And this did cost a lot of time and money. Not astonishing that the young engineers after graduation often say that *"They saw the light in the prototype module"* (quote from alumnus Robert Capel). They are other students after their prototype stands: more serious, more conscious, more aware of the role of creativity and their own precision in the material world of technology. They learned that all elements never fit automatically like one supposes after having had only the experiences of computer drawing. On paper tolerances do not exist. But in practice tolerances govern all assemblies. And they are proud of their own prototypes.

It is obvious that this study module is quite expensive for an architectural faculty. Apart from the high costs of laboratory, machinery and a permanent laboratory worker the material costs for all the standard, special and extravagant prototype elements are high and have to be enabled by industrial sponsoring.

Objects that the students typically make are façade component mock-ups, for instance of a double glass façade with movable elements. But one-offs are produced as well, for instance a tower with four different materials and four levels as well as a laboratory office with a giant glass door of 3 x 3.5 m. Assistant professor Peter van Swieten headed the laboratory for 15 years and we wrote a book on the Prototype Laboratory together. In 2015, Dr. Marcel Bilow took over Prototype Lab which is now called 'the Bucky Lab'. For me, the most memorable student prototype was the Maison d'Artiste which is explained hereafter as it entailed some intriguing glass challenges.

MAISON D'ARTISTE PROTOTYPE

In 2003, a group of laboratory students made a prototype for a reconstruction of the famous Maison d'Artiste designed by Theo van Doesburg and Cornelis van Eesteren at the beginning of De Stijl movement in 1923. The original design was published as a cardboard model at the scale 1 to 50 in the exhibition 'L'Effort Moderne' in Paris. It remained only a model and had never been built. The model was lost within one year after that and only eight black-and-white photographs remained in Dutch museums. However, these photographs of the model were published in many books on the history of architectural Modernism. The lost design had a major influence on architecture.

One group of second year students under leadership of student Joris Braat reconstructed a 3D model from the eight black-and-white photographs conserved in the Central Museum of Utrecht. These photographs had been taken mostly from the sides of the original cardboard model, and there was one showing the bottom (the model held upside down). Joris Braat and the students researched the original dimensions of the model with great accuracy. These measurements showed differences up to 15 % from previous reconstructions in the 1980s. For most of the planes this resulted in other proportions. We assumed 99% accuracy.

In the same atelier of students, Monique Suttorp reconstructed with a small group under leadership of student Cindy Beckers the colours in the model from the black-and-white photographs via an American colour spectograph and by researching the original Talens colours from 1923. This was even more of an experiment than the reconstruction of the geometry. This colour reconstruction study had, we assume, an accuracy of roughly 70 to 80 %. The colours were completely different from what models up until then (Veldhuijzen van Zanten) had shown. Most interesting was the staircase, which was reconstructed as bright red instead of the black colour that had been assumed in the 1980s. This was a strong indication of the influence exerted by the painter Van Doesburg and not by architect Van Eesteren. The entire colour composition was completely different, but breathed

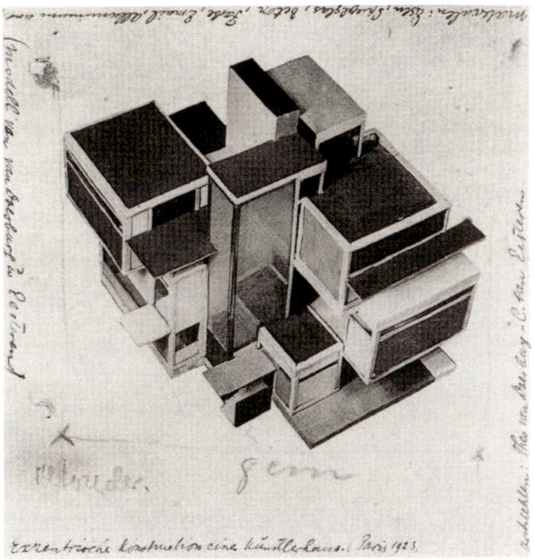

Fig. 39 Maison d'Artiste, original black and white photograph of the 1923 model.

Van Doesburg's spirit of living in a three-dimensional painting, so to speak.

After this study the group continued in their third year with shop drawings for a 1 to 5 scale model and one year later the same students built the 1 to 5 model themselves, composed of 18 different volumes in the Prototype Laboratory.

The reconstruction of the original dimensions and colour composition of the Maison d' Artiste design was a valuable contribution of the TU Delft students toward a better understanding of architectural history. Their model at a scale of 1 to 5 was positioned just outside the entrance of the former TU Delft Architecture building, which was completely destroyed by fire in 2008. But the day after the fire I was able to save the prototype from the debris. It has been restored, taken over by the 'Foundation Maison d'Artiste Prototype' and is now positioned at the TU Delft

Fig. 40 Cover of publication Reconstruction and Development of the Maison d'Artiste Prototype, 2017

campus. It was on display in Leiden during the exhibition '100 Years After De Stijl' in the summer of 2017. On this occasion the white model was displayed together with the documentation of the reconstructed colour composition. These achievements are documented in the book Reconstruction and Development of the Maison d'Artiste Prototype, 2017, [ref. 14].

It is rare to see second year student work that becomes a serious research & development contribution, worthwhile including in a major exhibition.
This research & development work posed two intriguing technical glass challenges: the glass façade of the atelier, 7 × 7 m in size and the three glass walls on which two storeys of the Maison are resting.

The glass façade of the atelier has been made in the 1923 model as one plane, logical for the 1 to 50 size of the model, in which the pane measures 140 x 140 mm. Float glass as the currently known flat glass was introduced only in 1959.

Fig. 41 Maison d'Artiste. Colour reconstruction by students of TU Delft, 2003.

But it was only in 2017, when Apple ordered maximum-sized glass panels for their new headquarters in Cupertino, California, that the size of available glass panels has increased considerably.

At this moment it is not yet possible to obtain 6.85 x 6.85 m panels as they can neither be produced nor transported. But half-sized panels are available, that is 3.425 x 6.850 m in single glass or double glass panels, laminated and also coated for solar admission of energy emission in winter. Subdivided into two 6.850 m high panels, 3.425 m wide. These panels could even be produced without any metal profile in the centre between the two vertical panels. The glass panel can be analyzed and dimensioned with one long free side in the centre and three sides of the panels fixed on the building using the current norms. The perimeter glazing system has to allow for putting in the large glass panels from the outside.

The three glass walls of the garden room or reception room ideally would have no corner columns to offer a free view to the outside. In a 1 to 100 model this is quite different from reality where the piano room and on top of that the master bedroom would be cantilevered from the central core. In case the upper two modules were made of reinforced concrete the combined dead and live loads would of course be much higher than in case of a lightweight steel frame with rigidly connected corners and extreme lightweight sandwich panels for the floors, roofs and outside façades. If executed in structural glass, a thick inner pane, triple laminated for safety, and connected via a spacer and an outside laminated pane with the necessary coatings, could be developed to withstand the vertical loadings from the upper storeys and yet be fully transparent. The glass thickness would have to be more than 50 mm and low-iron glass should be used, with minimal deflection due to its thickness. This would be the state-of-the-art glass technology available in 2020 for an eventual realization of the Maison d'Artiste. In that case the upper two storeys with piano room and master bedroom would hover over a large 9 m cantilever.

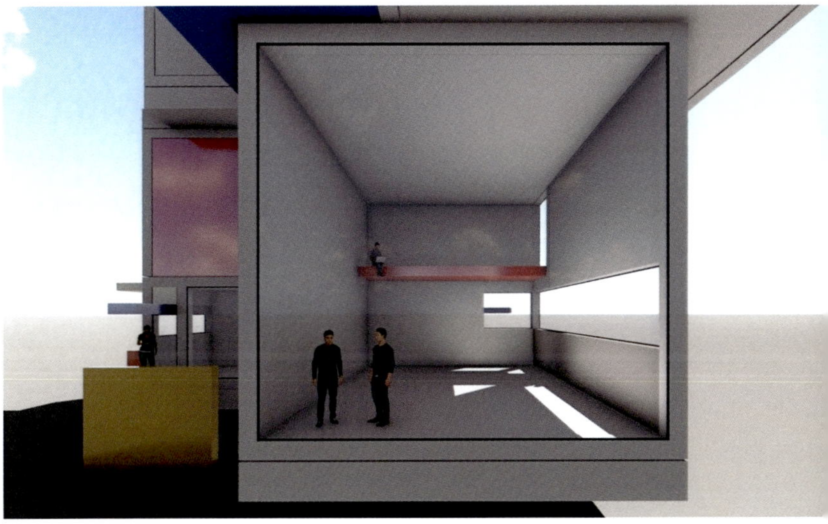

Fig. 42 The living room on the ground floor is surrounded by pure glass panes; they carry the loads of the piano room and the guest room on top, Tim van Beukering.

Fig. 43 In the Maison d'Artiste the atelier space has an enormous window pane of 7 × 7 m, Tim van Beukering.

Fig. 44 Model of Maison d' Artiste, scale 1 to 5, outside the former Architecture building at TU Delft up to the Day of the Great Fire May 13th 2008.

Fig. 45 Maison d'Artiste in full (reconstructed) colours as a part of the outdoor exhibition '100 Years After De Stijl', organized by the museum De Lakenhal, Leiden, 2017.

CHAPTER 1.5

From Existing Systems to Innovating Glazing Systems

The development of new materials, new components and new subsystems and systems for buildings falls into the domain of building product designers or component architects. An example of this work is the group Booosting, a Dutch association of technical architects, designers and industry to stimulate industrial building components; www.Booosting.nl. The most exciting times for a product designer are when he or she can design and develop something new. Yet one should not neglect the potential of the existing, as the efficiency of the building industry is in adaptation of the existing product, remembering Wittgenstein's proposition 4.65, 1923 [see page 25]. Existing systems once were new and experimental and then were duplicated and adapted. And after a number of applications under different circumstances the initial experiment becomes a system: pre-designed and pre-developed, ready to be finalized for different applications. And so experimental systems become finally established product systems in the building industry. However, there are also a number of examples that experimented successfully with available systems which then led to system improvements.

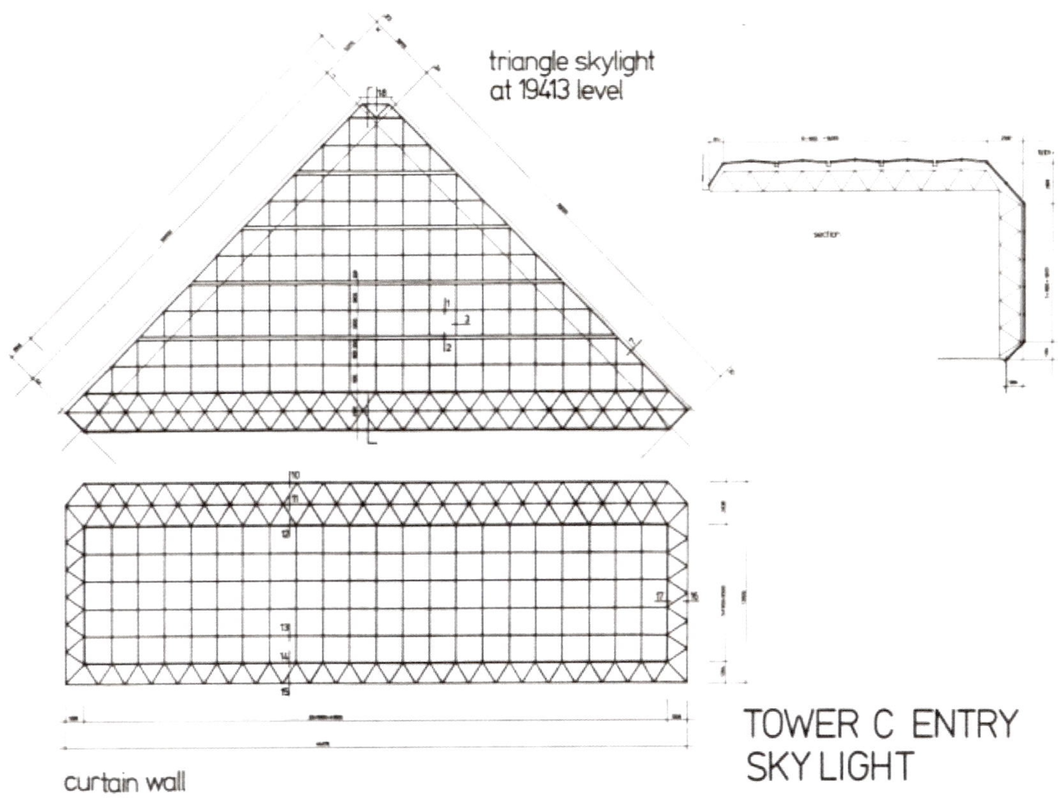

Fig. 48 Plan, elevation and cross section of the space frame with skylight of Raffles City.

Opposite page: Figs. 46, 47 Interior of the space frames and the skylight system for Raffles City, Singapore, 1986, architect I. M. Pei.

SKYLIGHTS FOR RAFFLES CITY

The skylights on top of the atrium space frames in the Raffles City project in Singapore had to be engineered and constructed according to the design of I. M. Pei, New York. In the early 1970s, I. M. Pei suffered through the problems with the John Hancock Tower in Boston (now 200 Clarendon Street), completed in 1976, where several glass panels fell off due to wind loads and where one side was structurally unstable and had to be retrofitted. It became facetiously known as the 'Plywood Palace' or 'Plywood Skyscraper' (Fig. 96) as the missing glass panels were temporarily replaced by plywood. Pei came out of that crisis with a strong façade advisory department under the lead of Fritz Sulzer. The challenge at Raffles City was: if one could develop a watertight skylight system in Singapore with its enormous sudden gusts of rain water, it would perform everywhere in the world adequately.

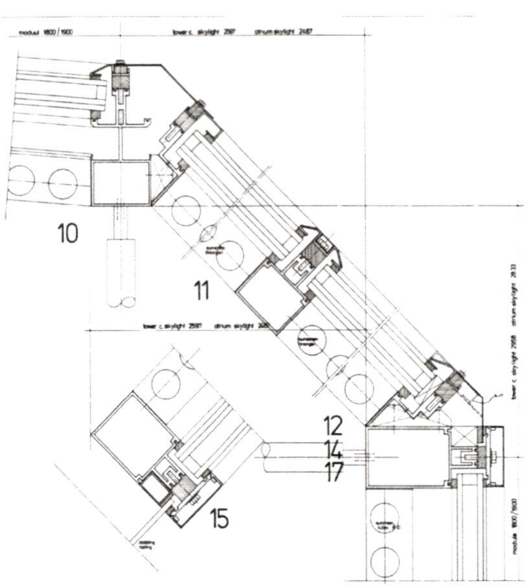

Fig. 49 Typical details of the skylight system for Raffles City (bespoke Kawneer system).

Watertightness and (temporary) rain water storage were the biggest issues to be resolved.

The lining of the aluminium mullions had been determined by the design of the architect and their position could not be altered. The skylight covered space frames, also the sloped, triangulated sides of the space frames did so. Hence the skylight had to follow the square lining of the space frame top members as well as the triangulated lining of the diagonals. This Raffles City skylight system, like any sensible aluminium-and-glass skylight system, is designed and developed with an internal drainage system. The basic idea is that all skylights once in their lifetime leak and that the leakage water has to be caught in different internal levels, cascading down from the highest level to the lowest level, sprouting out just above the gutter or a watertight flashing. The different aluminium profiles had to be engineered to fit, after properly machining the ends, into each other and to drain water safely and without any leakage from the highest level to the lowest level. In rectangular systems it is easy to choose the continuous profiles on the side of which perpendicular profiles are cut and machined in such a way that they fit in sidewards and drain off in the continuous profile. Normally three levels are identified: the top level, the crossing level and the collecting level.

But especially in the triangulated parts of the space frame where the roof plane is a steepy slope and all aluminium profiles are positioned sidewards, the integration of three levels was not that easily attained. The solution was found in a system where only one profile would run through and the other two had (after proper machining) to run into the continuous profile and also into one another as the sloping of all profiles sidewards required this (see fig 58-59) . It culminated in highly complicated aluminium mullion engineering, usually done by the engineering department of the aluminium profile supplier. However, their ingenuity had limits. So engineering this system with the aid of the German branch of Kawneer, producer of aluminium profile systems, became quite a challenge for Octatube, still a young engineering firm in 1982. The resulting system was complex and required high accuracies, local watertightness testing and highly skilled labour on site. The building site was at 30 m height, surrounded by four high towers under construction, manned by 500 Korean construction workers who occasionally threw down bolts or rubbish. So it turned out to be a dangerous building site, which had to be protected by a plywood roof layer on top of the glass plane of the roof.

Little did I suspect that this design and engineering exercise would become the entrance to a whole new world for Octatube and that it would mark the transition from designing space frame structures to designing glass structures and structural glass. Currently the roofs are well-maintained and in excellent shape, as seen during my last visit in Singapore December 2019.

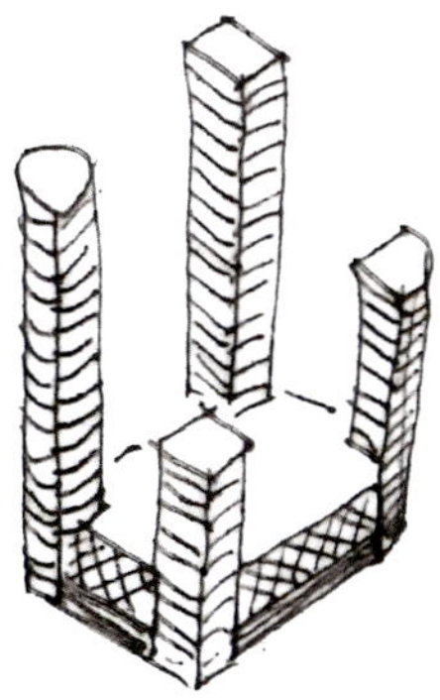

Fig. 50 Overall scheme of Raffles City complex with four 200 m high towers on a 30 m high basement with space frames and skylights.

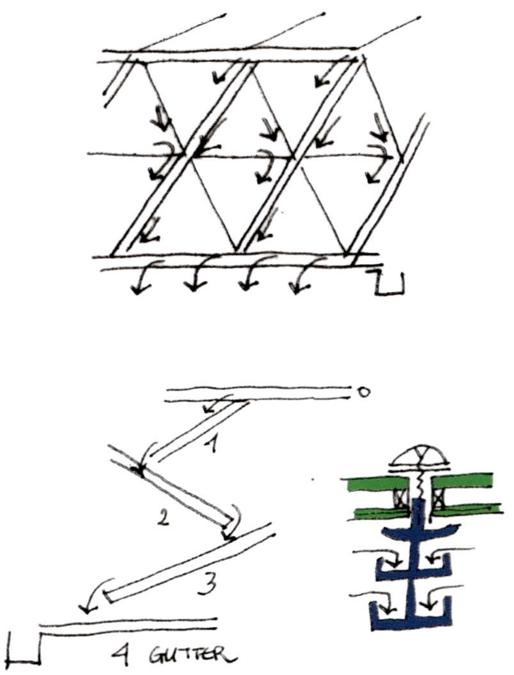

Fig. 51 Flow of drainage water from tertiary to secondary to primary levels down to the gutter. Below: Cascading of the internal leakage water levels.

ENTRANCE CANOPY RAFFLES CITY

The Tuball-Plus system is another example of an improved existing system . The existing Tuball system had to be developed further as the requirement from I. M. Pei for a canopy in Raffles City required an abstract system, much more abstract space frame than the mechanical Octatube system with visual bolts. The first step was to develop an abstract space frame system. Octatube's most important international competitor for space frames was Mero, based in Würzburg, Germany. The Mero system consisted of solid spheres in which bolts are screwed from the outside inwards. The new system had to be different. Thus we developed a system for the entrance canopy consisting of hollow spheres with the bolts to be screwed into the head side of the tubular members from the inside of the hollow sphere outwards. The inside of the sphere, which was divided in a ¾ shell and a ¼ cap, has no facets, so the bolts had to be provided with thick counter saucers under the bolt heads. The top of the tubular elements is made with a prop of cylindrical steel, machined to fit into the top of the tube, with a recess of 5 mm for the smaller tubes and subsequently welded on the inside rim, not visible from the outside. Bolt holes in the node could easily be drilled straight. The cap can be bolted on the shell by a central Allen-type bolt, from the top down for lower chord nodes, out of sight. In other cases, this bolt can be inserted and fixed from the bottom upward, like in top layers of space frames. This space frame system was developed to be made in aluminium as well as in steel, with diameters following the diameters of the tubes: 110 mm, 135 mm, 162 mm as the normal range. The spheres are cast in aluminium or in grey cast iron and are machined smooth before drilling the holes, then galvanized and powder-coated later.

For the two projects of 1983, the entrance canopy of Raffles and the Haarlem Music dome, glass panels had to be fixed in line with the space frame. The canopy of Raffles City consisted of an upper plane of squares and four sides of triangles. The top plane and the four sides are seen as a repetition of squares and triangles. The glass panels were glued structurally with

Figs. 52, 53 Interior and exterior of the entrance canopy of Raffles City.

silicone on top of the T-tops of the Tuball plus profiles. The individual laminated glass panels have only butt silicone joints for water tightening and form one reflective plane.

MUSIC PAVILION, HAARLEM

The Haarlem Music Dome was a polygon composed of three different triangles derived from a three-frequency icosahedron, as popularized by Richard Buckminster Fuller. In this case, the structural design consisted of a single-layered aluminium Tuball space frame where the glass panels were to be fixed on the tubular elements by a continuous T-profile, extruded in one procedure with the structural tube.

The design concept of the Haarlem was developed by architect Wiek Röling in a model with hexagons and pentagons. A dome-shaped space frame had to be made with similar components as the flat space frame of the entrance canopy at Raffles City. The design consisted of a sphere as the joint and of a circular tube as the structural bar. For the construction of the glass panels covering both the flat space frame in Singapore as well as the polygonal space frame in Haarlem, an O-T profile was designed. The O was the structural part in cross section, the tube, and the T provided the flat surface for accommodating the glass panels. The lower part of the T obstructed the mounting of the ¼ cap on the ¾ sphere. The cap had to be taken off and on during assembly. The Eureka moment came with the idea to machine the vertical flange of the T profile away in a semi-circular model. The connection of more bars on one node gave the connection detail a flower-like appearance. (Figs. 57, 58)

Fig. 54 Exterior of the Music Pavilion, Haarlem, 1983, architect Wiek Röling.

Fig. 55 Exterior detail with laminated, fully tempered glass panels, silicone-sealed after 2004.

Fig. 56 Interior of the Music Pavilion, Haarlem.

These two Tuball projects were the first ones where glass panels had to be tailored around the space frames. In both cases laminated annealed glass was used. In Haarlem, the 6 mm thick glass panels were composed of two 3 mm thick panes (referred to 3.3.1 by the glass industry) and were fixed by linear bolted strips as was typical in those days. For the Singapore project silicone sealing of the joints between the glass edges and the aluminium O-T-profiles and the butt joints glass-to-glass were considered. I. M. Pei was convinced we should experiment with silicone gluing of the glass panels this way. The silicone connection was known from structural glazing where a two-component silicone sealant forms the connection between the outer glass panels, covering the entire aluminium frame and the frame.

Usually the glass panes have a coated edge so that the aluminium profiles are not visible from the outside as they are covered with a black screening on the inside of the glass panel. This technology was transferred to the space frame system. The difference was, though, that the glass panels had to be fixed on site, not in the factory, where the production circumstances supply a dry working environment. The building sites in Singapore are wet because of frequent rains and a 90 % humidity. So, in retrospect, this first all-glued application of glazing could be described as somewhat naive. But it worked. After completion, the long canopy seemed to be covered by one large glass panel and was very abstract in its appearance. Since 1986 not a single panels broke or had to be substituted.

In Haarlem the flower-like detail gave the aluminium dome a romantic atmosphere. As it turned out, the Haarlem Music Pavilion had lousy acoustics as the dome form concentrated all sounds in the centre and it was impossible to use for concerts. The orchestra members had to stand on the perimeter of the floor in order to perform. Nevertheless, the design was rewarded with the first Dutch Aluminium Award of 1984. It frequently served as a background for marriage photographs and even was described in a novel of Dutch literature. Literature is even more eternal than architecture. Flemish poet Herwig Verleijen, wrote: *"Beitel mijn naam in het hardste marmer en nog wist de tijd hem uit, fluister hem als een gedicht en hij blijft eeuwig". ["Chisel my name in the toughest marble and yet time will erase it, whisper it in a poem and it stays forever"].*
The small music dome was definitely a contribution to culture.

The Tuball space frame system, invented in 1983 and applied in Singapore and Haarlem, was later used to cover thousands of square metres in projects all over the world. The largest one was a double Boeing 747 maintenance hangar in Mumbay, India, for Air India with 130 × 80 m free span. So small-scale experiments can lead to large-scale applications.

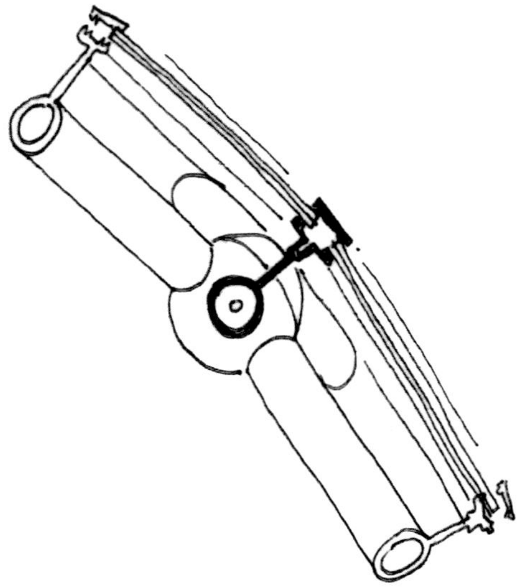

Fig. 57 Hand sketch of the Tuball-Plus detail with laminated annealed glass and continuous screw strips for the Haarlem Music Pavilion, 1983.

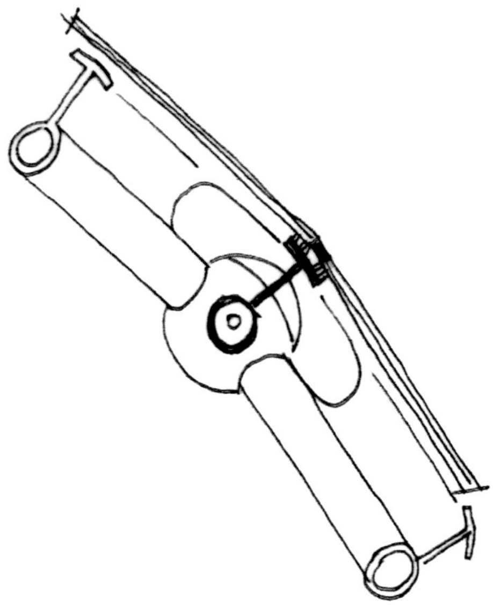

Fig. 58 The improved silicone-sealed Tuball system of 2005 with fully tempered glass (on top) used only a few clamps and laminated, fully tempered glass.

CHAPTER 2.
PLAY OF FORCES IN GLASS PANELS

Loads on glass panels in façades usually come from horizontal wind which results in bending stresses. Roof glazing has to absorb loads by snow and deadweight on bending. In the 1970s it was the full chemical edge sealant which was unusual, therefore structural glazing is referred to by the curtail wall industry as 'silicone-glued glazing' which means that the aluminium profiles are bonded by two-component silicone to the glass panels in the factory.

A seminal moment in the development of structural glazing was the design by the late Peter Rice of RFR in 1986 for the Serres of the Cité des Sciences et de l'Industrie at La Villette, Paris (architect Adrien Fainsilber). Glass panels were suspended and loaded by the deadweight of the lower panels: hence these panels were mainly loaded on tension by deadweight and local bending because of the more or less horizontal wind loading. This structure did not need any deadweight suspenders. Vertical deadweight forces were transferred to the upper steel tubes above each row of four panels by the glass panels itself. Wind forces were transferred by horizontal pre-stressed stainless steel cable trusses, using typical H-form stainless steel connectors. This project illuminated at the time a promising way of innovation. But the price of this frameless glass façade was twice as high as the average price affordable in the Netherlands. So for high tech architects in the Netherlands a more economical alternative had to be developed. How to take up that challenge?

Fig. 68 Cité des Sciences et de l'Industrie with the suspended glass system as designed by Peter Rice, Martin Francis and Ian Ritchie.

Fig. 69 Serre of Cité des Sciences et de l'Industrie, La Villette, Paris, 1986, architect Adrien Fainsilber.

Opposite page: Fig. 67 Exterior façade of Finsbury Pavement, London, 1997, architect Sheppard Robson.

CHAPTER 2.1
Play of Mainly Tension

Fig. 70 Structural prototype of an integral glass panel composition scale 1 to 3 by civil engineering student Rik Grashoff in 1988.

The publications of the glass serres of la Villette in Paris sparked an analysis. The glazing system was admired in its audacity, but the published m² costs were not feasible for the Dutch market. An adaptation of the structural system resulting in a more economic price had to be pursued. The structural system puzzled many glass engineers. In this case academia came to the rescue of the development in industry in the form of an experimental graduation project.

FIRST GLASS ASSEMBLIES

Civil Engineering student Rik Grashoff, became later member of the Dutch parliament, developed at Octatube a system of combining nine panes of 2 x 2 m each into one big glass panel of 6 × 6 m by means of bolted and pre-stressed connectors and cables. A mechanical step forwards, not aesthetically pleasing yet, but breaking ground.

Figs. 71, 72 First application of an integral glass structure with square glass panels of 2 × 2 m at shop Cool Cat, Groningen, 1989, architect Paul Verheij. Façade exterior and Quattro node detail.

Rik Grashoff's proposal started the in-house developments at Octatube in the realm of structural glass façades and roofs. His model was shown at the first Booosting exhibition in November 1988. The comments were that the principle opened up new horizons, but that its aesthetic appearance needed improvement.

Immediately after publication of this prototype architect Paul Verheij contacted Octatube and we designed a 4 m high and 6 m wide glass façade whose panels were connected without a frame, as before, but more elegant. The entire glass panel ensemble was to be suspended from the upper lugs, and the surrounding edge connectors acted as stabilization against wind loading. The lower connector even had sleeve holes not to have the deadweight of the bridge as an extra load on the glass ensemble. Thus shop front for Cool Cat in Groningen received quite harmonious proportions.

From then onwards an incremental development route was chosen for structural systems in glass, all of them were very experimental at the time. The first project in Amsterdam focussed on tension and bending in glass, followed by a project in Eindhoven on compression and bending the glass panels, see fig 83, 84.

GLASS MUSIC HALL, AMSTERDAM

A few weeks after the publication of Rik Grashoff's experimental model at the Booosting exhibition, architect Pieter Zaanen phoned and suggested a use of this principle for his transparent concert hall in the Grain Hall of the famous Stock Exchange by Hendrik Berlage in Amsterdam, built in 1903. Based on the principle of suspended glass panel assemblies, a principle design was conceived for a glass volume of 10 × 10 × 20 m, an upside-down aquarium. The box consists of a roof steel construction supported by columns and glass façades suspended from the roof, all independent of the existing building. The glass concert hall was to house chamber orchestra performances and rehearsals.

Fig. 73 Glass Music Hall, Amsterdam, 1989, model scale 1 to 50 [ref.15].

The acoustics had to be developed simultaneously; acoustical elements that reflect or absorb sound had to be integrated. It took half a year of concept development and fundraising before the design could be finalized. The steel roof structure subsequently became a standard steel Tuball space frame on six vertical slender columns. The space frame was stiff enough so that in the facades the glass could be suspended from it. The glass music hall was inaugurated in spring 1990. The final dimensions of the hall were 9 to 13 m wide, 9 m high and 22 m long. The glass panels were suspended from the roof structure, five panels, each 1.8 m high. Glass panels were only 8 mm thin. The glass was fully tempered. Stabilization was attained by super slender steel tensile trusses of 10 mm thick solid rods. These slender dimensions could be achieved because the glass hall is inside of a building and thus not exposed to wind loads or snow loads on the roof. Neither were watertightness problems to be expected since rain would only occur in an outside situation. The wind pressure calculated for was only 30N/m², caused by overpressure or underpressure of the ventilation system. The stabilization system and the panels loaded on tension were already experimental enough.

Zaanen wanted a completely independent glass volume to serve as the acoustical envelope for concerts for 200 visitors and rehearsals for a 20 men chamber music orchestra. The 8 mm thin glass proved to meet the required acoustical reduction of 25 dB. Acoustical advisor was Rob Metkemeijer of Peutz Associés. Despite the hard (and thus sound-reflecting) surfaces of the glass, good internal acoustics were achieved by means of perforated sound-absorbing metal components suspended on the inside and from the acrylic domes in the ceiling, which were suspended up and down, distributing sound to all sides.

The Amsterdam Glass Music Hall was an experiment as far as the structural use of glass was concerned as this had not been done before in the Netherlands. In this case the idea was to load the glass panels in tension only, by the deadweight of the lower glass panels. The façade was really a suspended curtain where all upper panels carried the deadweight of the lower panels. And in order to stabilize these panels against horizontal loadings like overpressure the façade needed a minimal, pre-stressed tensile truss of 10 mm steel rods, on which welded Quattro nodes were screwed that were connected to the glass panels. The tensile truss was stressed between a stiff upper structure and a stiff lower structure. This upper structure was a space frame and the lower structure was the reinforced concrete floor slab. Thus deadweight and horizontal loadings were dealt with separately.

During the construction phase in late 1989, the upper panels were hung first, then the second, third and fourth row. When all these panels were in place and prior to the installation of the lowest and fifth row of panels, the phenomenon of progressive collapse was discussed. What would happen when an upper panel broke? It was determined to break one of the upper panels deliberately, in order to understand whether a progressive collapse would occur. The panel connections were

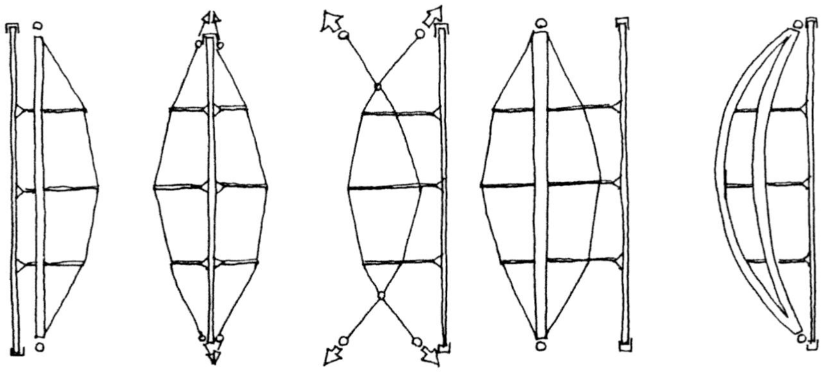

Fig. 74 Different schemes for open and autonomous supporting steel structures with cables as tensile elements.

dimensioned for double loadings and, indeed, after an unexpectedly rude treatment of one glass panel by a glass installer, one upper panel broke with a big explosion (as it was a highly pre-stressed glass), but the lower panels remained intact and in position. Octatube was relieved and so was the client. In later respect this Glass Music Hall appeared to become the historical predecessor first of many Zappi adventures, which would start in 1992.

The glass music hall has three straight façades, the fourth one is curved because of acoustical considerations, to reduce flutter between parallel planes. Architect Zaanen agreed with giving the three façades a tensile character and to stabilize the curved façade by the use of circular tubes (CHS). This façade would be self-supporting and positioned somewhat apart from the space frame. The roof structure as a space frame is known for its rigidity. The upper space frame structure was lightweight and yet rigid enough to span between roof and floor structure by means of vertical tensile trusses. The form of the tensile trusses was derived from bending moment lines and were to absorb horizontal loadings, in this case modest though, but nevertheless independent of the size of the loading. The logical form was two counter forming moment lines with low tensile forces in the tensile rods, see the central scheme in figure 74.

To exploit the differences between the straight façades and the curved one structurally, we proposed to have the curved façade in grey coated glass, so that the curved façade would be seen as a curved object. The architect, well-known for his work for theatres, suggested instead: *"Why don't we make the straight façade grey tinted glass and the curved façade transparent. Then you enter a black box and all of a sudden you see through a transparent curved façade."*

Fig. 75 Glass Music Hall. Full-size, welded Quattro connection detail with sandpaper washers to increase the friction between glass and steel surfaces through the pre-stress bolts.

Fig. 76 Interior of the Glass Music Hall.

Fig. 77 Exterior of the Glass Music Hall, Amsterdam, 1990, architect Pieter Zaanen [ref.15].

That was also the reason the hall was eventually slightly twisted in position in the existing plan, i.e. not parallel with the perimeter walls of the Berlage building. These two maneuvers gave a technical artifact a much more theatrical quality; they created tension and romance.

This very first of structural glass applications in the Netherlands was a careful step ahead in the sense of the bolted connections. Two bolt connection types are known from mechanical engineering: the shear bolt (shear forces through the side of the glass hole and the stem of the bolt) and pre-stressed bolts (in larger holes, where the pre-stress in the bolt produces compression on the glass panels by the surface friction). Tests on the different types of bolts on glass pales showed that friction bolts produced a higher connection force. Yet the deadweight of the glass panes (multiplied by two as one of the adjacent panels could explode) was too high for the glass surface friction. One-sided sand paper washers were introduced with the sandpaper side turned towards the glass. This produced the desired friction surface, which was proven by tests. This, of course, was only possible in indoor applications, and not outside as the sandpaper would erode by water ingress and frost. Nowadays, however, this problem would be resolved by gluing stainless steel washers to the glass surface around the bolt holes and use shear bolts. In 2014, the Glass Music Hall was dismantled because the management of the Beurs van Berlage wanted to use the Grain Hall for larger numbers of visitors and the NedPhO had found alternative accommodation in Amsterdam (Gerardus Majellakerk or the NedPhO cupola). Thanks to Kees Spanjers, Pieter Zaanen's successor, the management of the Beurs van Berlage agreed to dismantle and reuse the building instead of demolishing and removing it. The Glass Music Hall was reassembled five years later in the LocHal of Tilburg in exactly the same arrangement, with its famous excellent acoustics. It was recognised as a sign of great durability. The LocHal received international recognition as 'The best BNA building of 2019'.

THREE MORE GLASS CONCERT HALLS

Subsequently, three more glass concert halls, all with good acoustics, were developed with the same acoustical engineer, Rob Metkemeijer: The Nieuwe Kerk in The Hague, the Glass Museum Hall in the Prinsenhof Museum, Delft and the Glass Synagogue Hall, The Hague, all shown in this book. In all four music halls glass panels enclose the concert area. The sound reflections off the hard glass surfaces were balanced by absorption in acoustical panels, normally heavily perforated metal panels filled with glass or rock wool. In other cases large openings were used to allow sound to disappear.

The suspended glass structure of the Nieuwe Kerk, built in 1656, served to shorten the acoustical reverberation time dramatically from 5 seconds to around 1.5 seconds, which was necessary in the transition from a church whose interior was conceived for organ music and multi-vocal singing to an interior suitable for speech and chamber orchestra music. The church volume is 17.000 m3. The half open inner hall has a volume of 3.000 m3. The glass envelope consists of glass curtains and glass ceilings, architect Kees Spanjers. The ceilings are suspended at a height of 10 m from new steel arches just below the timber roof structure. The glass curtains are hung at 10 m height and have their lower sides at about 3 m, so that people can walk on the complete ground floor without any obstructions. The glass curtains are suspended from curved steel tubes and form a curve, the panels are connected with Quattro nodes and have additional deadweight suspenders for extra safety. After installation of the acoustical glass envelope, alternative studies were made to bring the 18th century organ in full view again in order to be able to play organ concerts. The latest idea is to move the glass curtain in front of the organ suspended on a rail to left and right in two halves, realized in summer 2020.

Fig. 78 Interior of the Glass Music Hall in Amsterdam, 1990.

Fig. 79 Drawing of a suspended half open glass envelope for acoustical improvements in the Nieuwe Kerk, The Hague, architect Kees Spanjers, 1996.

Fig. 80 Interior of the Nieuwe Kerk of The Hague built in 1656 as one of the first protestant churches after the 80-year liberation war with Spain. The glass curtains and ceiling are hardly visible.

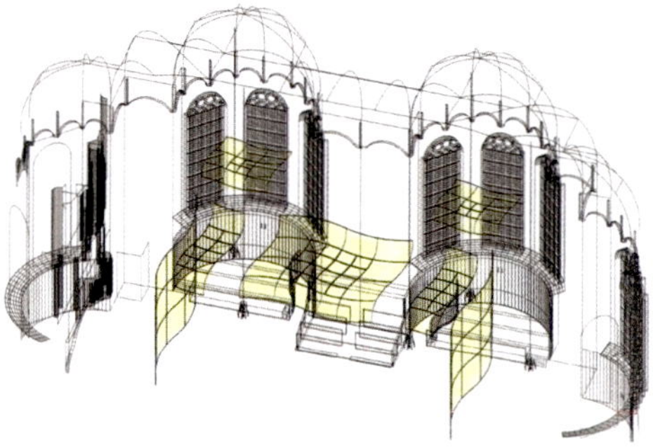

The glass curtains are suspended from crossing steel tubes and have an arched shape. The glass panels are connected to Quattro nodes and have extra vertical tie rods to safely carry the weight of the glass panels. After all, there are people underneath. At the time of the development of the glass inner hall (1996) the organ was no longer played.

After the restoration in 2019 of the Duyschot organ from 1702, the need arose to be able to give organ concerts again. Therefore the glass curtain in front of the organ was split in two halves that could be shifted sideways hanging on a rail and rotated at the end. In this way the 18th century baroque organ comes into full view again in order to be able to flush organ concerts. And to be admired again in full glory on Dutch Monument-days. (2020). The two half organ curtains can be rolled sideways on a rail in 3 positions: the closed concert stand, the half-open monument stand and the wide-open organ stand. The original curved glass, provided with a one-sided pvb foil, was completely re-used; the wooden reflectors were strongly rejuvenated at the back (slimming like turning a swimming costume into a bikini). The turning of the two glass screens at the end of the rail is particularly astonishing.

FLOWER SHOP ROOF IN HULST

In 1990, Dutch architect Walter Lockefeer contacted us with a vision for an invisible roof for a flower shop in Hulst in the Netherlands. He was an admirer of the Benedictine monk and architect Dom Hans van der Laan (1904–1991) with his influential architectural theory on numerical ratios in architecture.

It would again be part of 'Zappi avant la lettre'. He had designed two cubes with a rib size of 7.654 m of which only the walls in specially designed concrete blocks were to be visible. His concept was based on the observation that human beings, when standing upright in a space, perceive mainly the walls but hardly the floors and even to a lesser degree the ceiling. So the ceiling was to be "designed away", or "made invisible" [Ref. 17]. This was explained to me in a five-minute telephone conversation and this opportunity was seized immediately. The glass roof construction was made by forming a surrounding frame of RHS profiles. Between the corners a diagonal tensile web was engineered with vertical studs that took the loadings to the tensile members and directed them to the four corners of the frame, which was supported in the concrete block wall. The double glass panels were laid on top of the steel compression studs and glued to them (first time ever). The insulated glass panels (pre-stressed panes of 8 mm on top and laminated 2 x 6 mm in bottom layer) were so thick and heavy that uplift as a loading case was not to be expected.

For extra safety, a slight upward wind force was anticipated. So the Flower Shop filled in some of the technical blanks that the Glass Music Hall, completed earlier in the same year, had left.

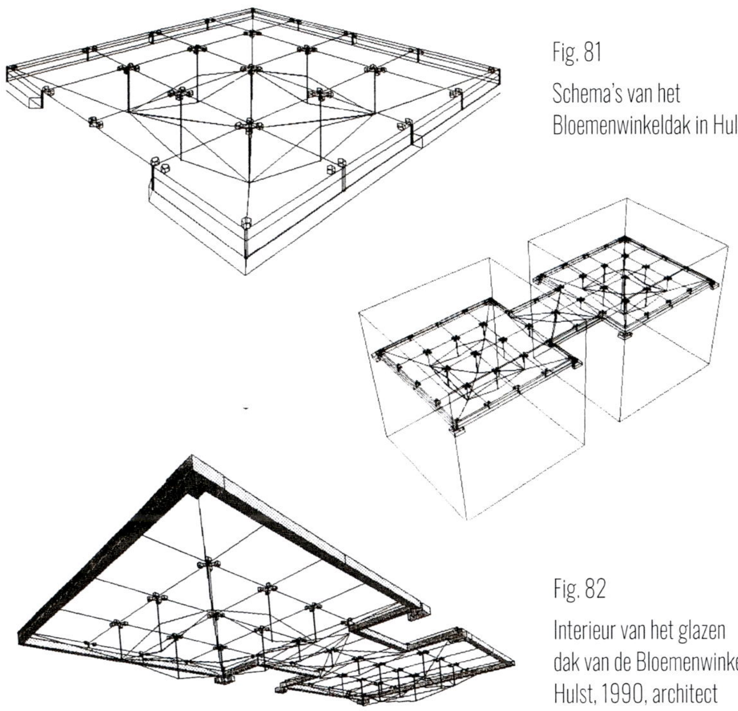

Fig. 81
Schema's van het Bloemenwinkeldak in Hulst.

Fig. 82
Interieur van het glazen dak van de Bloemenwinkel, Hulst, 1990, architect Walter Lockefeer.

CHAPTER 2.2

Play of Mainly Compression

The canopy of the Evoluon in Eindhoven was an experiment (1991) in compressed glass panels, post-stressed by a tensile rod system. The architect, Gert Grosveld, was inspired by the publication of a four-panel canopy we had made for the House of the Future in Rosmalen, designed by architect Cees Dam. He posed the question to us whether it would be possible to enlarge the same scheme of 4 × 4 m into 10 ×10 m, or 2 × 2 m panels into 5 × 5 m panels, quite a challenge! Our idea was to employ a vertical free-standing column or pillar. The glass panels had to be cantilevered on all four sides.

Fig. 83 Canopy of the Evoluon, Eindhoven, 1991, architect Gert Grosveld. By post-tensioning the spokes, the glass panels are automatically loaded with compression forces

Fig. 84 Connection details of canopy. All components were designed and engineered without CAD.

The result was a canopy, sized 10 × 10 m, composed of 25 glass panels that each measured 2 × 2 m. Some panels were cut on their diagonal to form the four drainage ridges in the roof. The main steel tubular structure resembles a tree, with cantilevering branches, from which then in turn the outer glass panels are cantilevered, stabilized by tensile spokes downwards and upwards. These tensile spokes introduce enough post-tension to generate compression as normal forces in the glass panels. The glass panels consisted of monolithic 10 mm fully tempered glass, tinted grey. Famous Dutch architect Gerrit Rietveld would have been jealous on the extreme thin roof edge.

In 1993/1994 the glass industry witnessed a turn in safety thinking, resulting in the general conviction that laminated heat-strengthened glass panels should be used for any overhead glazing. This was triggered by the failure of five glass panels in the monolithic overhead glazing at Waterloo Station in London, realized by Nicolas Grimshaw in 1994 and the legal cases thereafter. The glazing had to be replaced by laminated and heat-strengthened glass panels.

CHAPTER 2.3
Self-Stabilising Glass Structures

For the Erasmus Medical Centre Library in Rotterdam, architect Kees Kaan designed a 12 m high all-glass façade with glass panels adjacent to each other, under 45 degrees to the building and stabilizing each other perpendicularly much like a mouse ladder. In this façade, the glass panels form vertical rows that are 1.5 m wide, stacked on top of each other, and these vertical rows stabilize each other and create a zig-zag glass façade. In the corners, however, a square steel rod acts as a continuous tensile member and takes up tension forces in the façade. The tensile members are impossible to see from the inside nor from the outside. The project received the 'Rotterdam Architectuurprijs 2013'.

Figs. 85, 86, 87 Design, execution and overall view of the zig-zag façade of the Erasmus Medical Centre Library, Rotterdam, architect Kees Kaan, 2012.

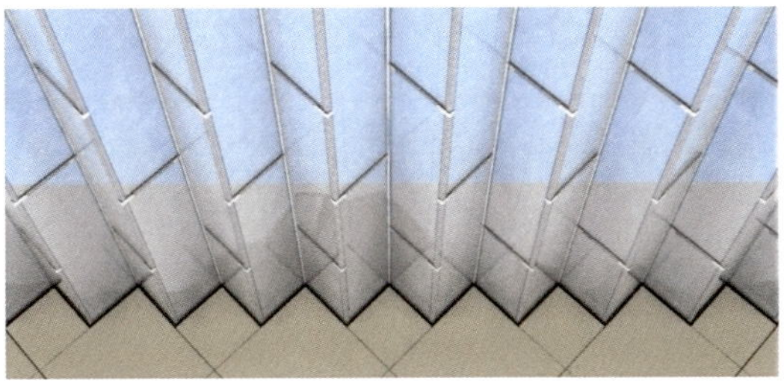

CHAPTER 2.4

Play of Compression and Tension

In 2002, Jan Wurm, at the time PhD student and research fellow at TU Delft, now Arup [ref.18], designed, engineered and built with the aid of students a prototype of an all-glass dome. The initial design proposal had been an asymmetrical dome, at least with an asymmetrical apex, see figure 89, but eventually a symmetrical set-up was chosen. He worked with five students on a frameless glass dome without steel structure or external/ internal nodes that was to have a shallow silhouette and a 20 m span in reality. The detailing was the main object of study. The prototype model had a scale of 1 to 5. The connections between the glass panels in the mock-up were executed in metal and had to be similar to the design detail for the full-size dome. The joints consisted primarily of glued connections of the metal strips with the glass panels. An actual dome would have insulated glass panels of which the laminated lower panes in heat-strengthened glass would get the developed frameless structural connection. The weather seal between the upper panes ensured complete watertightness for the structural joint in the sealant area. This experimental prototype was built and demounted several times since it was used for exhibitions. The last position of the 4 m dome was adjacent to the former building of Bouwkunde at TU Delft which burned down in May 2008. The dome model was lost.

Fig. 88 The 4 m diameter all-glass dome built as a prototype at TU Delft by research fellow and PhD student Jan Wurm and students in 2002.

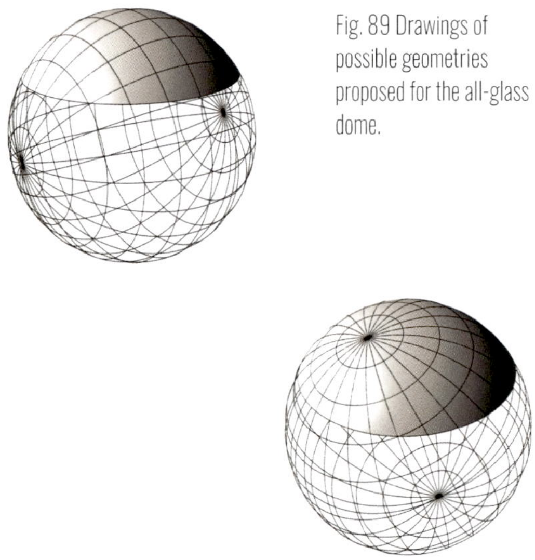

Fig. 89 Drawings of possible geometries proposed for the all-glass dome.

Fig. 90 The enlarged principle detail in 6 mm glass and small steel bars glued to the glass panels and bolted together.

The prototype stimulated a step forward. Five years later, in 2007, a full-size all-glass structure with insulated glass was designed by Architectenkamer for a mosque in Haarlem, the Netherlands. The 4 m high dome had a 8 m span. The idea was to make the dome self-supporting by its glass panels, without aluminium or steel framing, thus resembling an igloo. Similar to the prototype at TU Delft, the panels were triangular in form, the geometry a three-frequency icosahedron. The insulated, laminated glass panels had solar coating and low-E coatings. The glass panels were fixed to each other by hexagonal and pentagonal corner pieces. It was found that wind suction was prevalent, it would act like an inflated glass balloon. The usual dome is usually stressed by deadweights and snow loads combined resulting in compression forces downwards and tensile forces in the horizontal lower rings. Internally, in the space between the glass panels a tensile system of 8 mm thin stainless steel tensile rods was placed between the corner connectors, resulting in an invisible tensile cable network. This thin tensile network serves also for upward forces by wind loading. On both sides, the rods were sealed by silicone, also not visible. The structure appeared to be extremely vulnerable because of the initial positioning of the glass panels, stacked one on top of the other. Tolerances can be enlarged by the smallest corners. So the lower panels were positioned on a solid steel frame and auxiliary temporary supports on bottom scaffolding (later removed), and then assembled.

Fig. 91 Exterior of the Haarlem mosque with the all-glass dome on top, 2007, architect Architectenkamer.

Fig. 92 Interior of the Haarlem mosque with the transparent all-glass dome.

These two experiments (the dome at TU Delft and the Haarlem mosque) proved that indeed a shallow all-glass dome would be possible. As the connection from glass panel to glass panel would ensure a continuous glass surface, the subdivision would not matter. Triangulation, preferred for stability reasons in single-layered space frames, was not mandatory.
A rectangular form with trapezoidal subdivisions and an odd axis is an option as well. The advantage of a Schwedler type geometry (horizontal rings and radial legs) for a dome are an easier geometry, more rectangular panels and continuous tensile forces in the rings. But it is also a very logic and dull geometry.

The size of the flat panels influences local stability: small panels with their small corners more easily are prone to local snap-through due to perpendicular external loadings. A shear connection has to be used in between the four panels on four corners without the danger of rotating the nodes. The connection is preferably two-sided so that there are fewer bending moments acting on it. More rigidity could be attained when small tensegrity studs were connected to nodes at the inside, stabilizing a gently curved surface against local buckling. In addition to this structural connection, watertightness had to be achieved. My idea as a structural designer is that this design concept could be realized up to 12 to 15 m span.

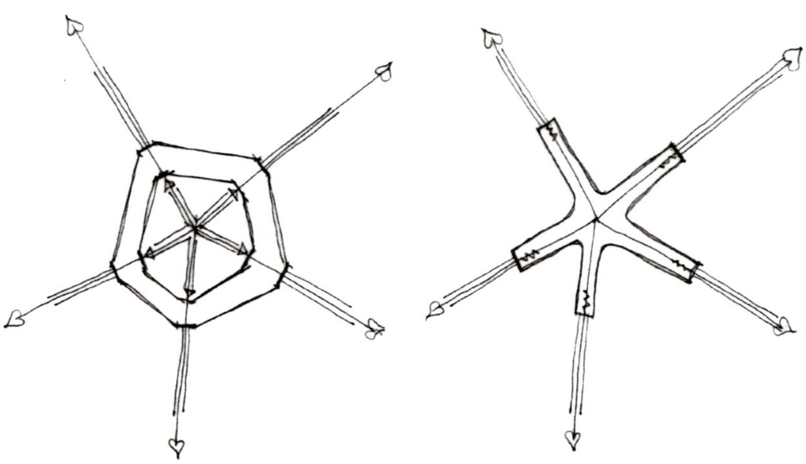

Fig. 93 Sketch of the glass panel connection at Haarlem Mosque

Fig. 94 Sketch proposal for improved and almost invisible connections in future projects: the pentagonal nodes could be replaced by finger-form nodes, with tensile nods in between them, under the silicone sealant. The nodes, if positioned on the outside, would be in the shadow of the spacer and the silicone sealant.

CHAPTER 2.5

Bending, Tension, Compression and Shear

In structural design of glass compositions we have dealt in the previous paragraphs with pure tension, pure compression, but bending forces (due to out-of-plane wind) and shear forces (due to in-plane forces) are frequently occurring for more complicated glass structures. When designing a glass roof beam the design comprises shear forces to bring the external loading from the roof plane in the glass material to the two supporting points at the end of the beam. After a long journey and several years, it was decided that multiple laminated glass beams are safe to build up to 12 to 15 m length. But they are quite expensive as there are only a few manufacturers in the world using pre-stress ovens and long laminating chambers. What to do when an architect wishes to make a larger span? Extensive knowledge was gained in the process of the Swiss Life project which is why we relate the full story here.

The cubical building for Swiss Life in Amstelveen, the Netherlands, has the shape of an H. The architect was Pi de Bruijn (ArchitectenCie) and the architectural engineer ABT. The two open tops of the building were to be closed off symbolically with glass beams, spanning 21 and 27 m at a height of 25 m. These gigantic glass beams or 'louvres' were free-spanning horizontally over 21 and 27 m and they were composed from glass panels 2 x 2 m, so with a height of 2 m. At the time of tender the glass composition was to be annealed triple glass, two panes of 6 mm and a central pane of 15 mm with 2 pvb foils between the glass panes. Annealed glass is not thermally pre-stressed and quite vulnerable for breakage, surely around the bolt holes for connecting the separate glass panels to a long entity. Octatube was the only subcontractor who dared to quote a price for engineering, development, production and installation of the glass structure. However, the structural composition was problematic and therefore a price was quoted based on an improved structural development, without taking over the design liability of the structural engineer. Thus the role of Octatube was essential here. The glass beams project seemed to me as the person who had to take all responsibility and liability, potentially dangerous. This glass beam contract turned into a development project, in which numerous laboratory tests were done. Alas, the experiments and tests proved that it was not yet feasible to build the glass beams. The designer had proposed triple annealed glass and glass as the main structural medium. After analysis by the structural engineers of Octatube, a long development process for the connection details was executed before it would have been possible to build the glass beams with a safety factor of 4. Quite early in the process, Octatube proposed an alternative solution: two parallel steel cables with a diameter of 20 mm as the main structural elements, instead of full glass, see figure 99. On a height of 25 m no one would be able to see the 20 mm steel cables.

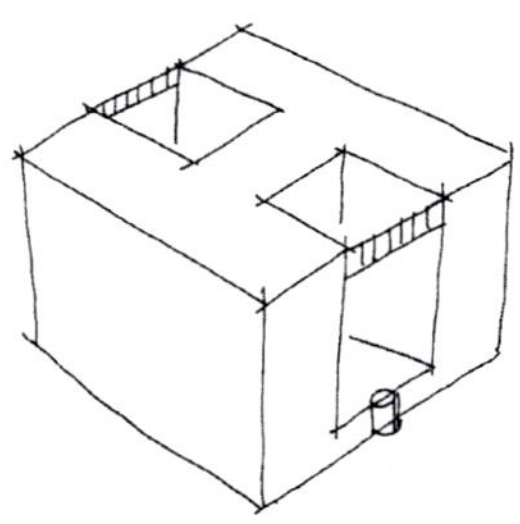

Fig. 95 Schematic drawing of Swiss Life Headquarters in Amstelveen with glass louvres.

Fig. 96 The John Hancock Tower in Boston, 1972, architect I. M. Pei that became known as the 'Plywood Skyscraper'.

Fig 97 The myth of the sword of Damocles, suspended above the chair of the king on only one horse's hair.

This scheme was neither accepted by the structural engineer nor by the architect. The proposal did not seem advanced enough in their eyes. And we proposed in vain to get a second opinion on the safety behaviour by a certified German 'Prüfungsingenieur' like prof. dr. Jörgen Wörner, then president of the Technische Universität in Darmstadt, with whom I discussed the proposal. For him there was only one solution: the proposed double load bearing cables and glass panels as infill. The entire structure would still be demanding enough attention and engineering energy in developing its stabilisers and connections. The development time was over three years and the total project budget was consumed by more than 80 % for tests up to the point that the architect Pi de Bruijn was convinced to have pursued an impossible dream. He was in fact a few years too early.

Entering unknown grounds with unknown consequences also played a part in the famous 'Plywood Skycraper', i.e. the John Hancock Tower in Boston. Just after completion of the building in 1972, several glass panels collapsed in the façade of this high rise. Why did those upper glass panels break? They caused several lower panels to be shattered on their way down. The open windows were filled with plywood, thus earning the building its nickname. Nobody had any idea what caused this problem and it haunted the entire profession. Only after two years of intensive research architect I. M. Pei understood the reason of the glass panels falling out. The steel structural skeleton was too flexible and the ground plan of the building was a parallelogram with uneven stiffness in torsion. The skeleton was kept, but a balancing instrument was added on top. The façades were properly designed, engineered, produced and installed. For a fully responsible and liable design & build

Fig. 98 Swiss Life Headquarters, Amstelveen, prior to installation of the glass louvres, architect Pi de Bruijn.

office such as Octatube the memory of the 'Plywood Skyscraper' served as a warning. For any engineer, venturing into unknown territory always evokes the famous sword of Damocles suspended from one horse hair above one's self.

Swiss Life has safety and carefree life in its blazon. Dutch advertisements of Swiss Life show two people driving a red Cadillac convertible in the Nevada desert to Las Vegas. How could safety be neglected in this Swiss life project? First step was to convince the engineer to use fully tempered glass. On the site, sample a fully tempered monolithic glass pane was suspended from a tower crane at 25 m height and deliberately broken. The so-called 'safety particles' shattered all over the place, but also plates or shells of particles fell down of half a meter in size, which made 50 mm deep grooves in the soil before collapsing into particles again. The falling down of glass shards of this size could be lethal! The second laminated panel was broken in one panel and became curved, no problem yet, Then the second pane was broken and after half an hour of tearing and breaking out the holes in the PVB film the twice broken glass panel occurred much like an autumn leaf zig-zagging in the air towards the ground. The message was clear: no glass panel must ever drop down, especially not above the main entrance and not from a height of 25 m! The composition of the two glass beams consisting of glass panels had to make sure that a panel could not break out of the technical ensemble of the glass beam, even when fully broken. The glass laminators refused at the time a laminate where double PVB films were reinforced by a thin stainless steel mesh, so that the mesh would prevent the glass panels from ever falling out of the bolted connections. Ten years later a metal mesh in the PVB laminate was accepted practice. The project engineer also did not allow development on the basis of glued connections.

Since none of these alternative schemes could be realized and since glued connections were not allowed, the detail development was focused on the bolted connections, which were direct shear bolts with large bolt holes and intermediate plastic material to distribute the high stresses on the glass edges. The glass louvres had horizontal stabilizations with outriggers and cables, which in principle were only a minor problem. The problem was posed by the vertical trajectory of forces inside the glass panels. The focus of our research was on the connections for routing the vertical forces of deadweight. Halfway the development a new question from the project designers was posed how to position a glass cleaning apparatus on top of the glass louvres. This would require quite a sturdy and visible rail. Not even a usual safely of use was conceived, mainly the play of forces. We left that challenge all along. After two years of vigorous detail testing, the maximum stresses to be measured were only 60 % of the maximum stresses with safety factor of 4. The structural engineer was satisfied with a lower safety factor of 2.4. However, the client did not want to take the risk. The final conclusion of Octatube was that the project was impossible to build under the conditions given.

A mock-up with the scale 1 to 2 was built in the Octatube laboratory, ready to be loaded with water to obtain true stress values in the glass connections. It was three years after the start of the contract, when the building was already inaugurated and occupied, that the client stopped these experiments.

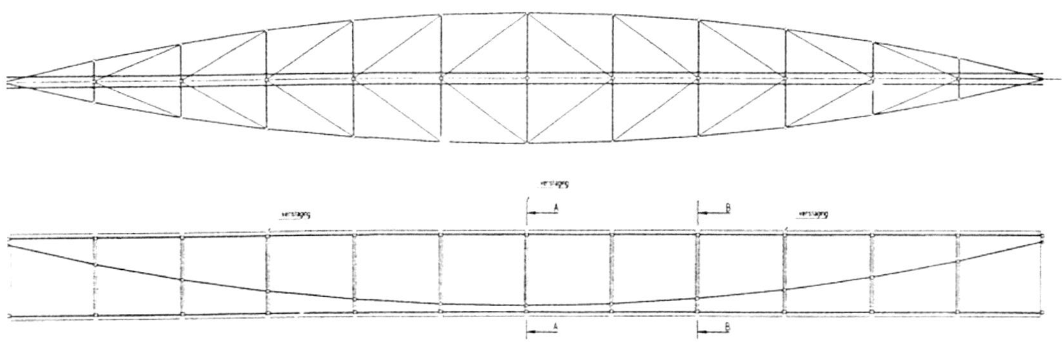

Fig. 99 Octatube's alternative proposal for the glass louvres with two suspended cables (diameter 20 mm) and non-loadbearing glass panels in between these cables.

Reflecting on this process in hindsight it is clear that the tender design with the glass louvres was not worked out completely. The design was not based on practical experience. It went too early to the market for tendering and left experimentation over to the subcontractor. His role was to take over the design & build responsibility. In such experimental cases both engineering parties need each other more than ever. At the time of engineering the design phase was not yet over. The better solution would have been to award the development of the louvres to a specialist-contractor long before the building design was sent out for tendering. So an appropriate experimentation prototype process was not foreseen in the design or the design was offered to early to the market.

It was only years later that I heard that the main contractor had been in legal process with the client on this subject.

However, the ABT-project engineer of Swiss Life, Rob Nijsse, later one of my colleagues at the Faculty of Architecture, describes the development of the project in his book Glass in Structures [ref. 19] from another point of view.

Fig. 100, 101 Mock-ups of the 27 m long glass beam on scale 1 to2 with full-scale details in the Octatube Laboratory, ready for full-scale loading by water basins.

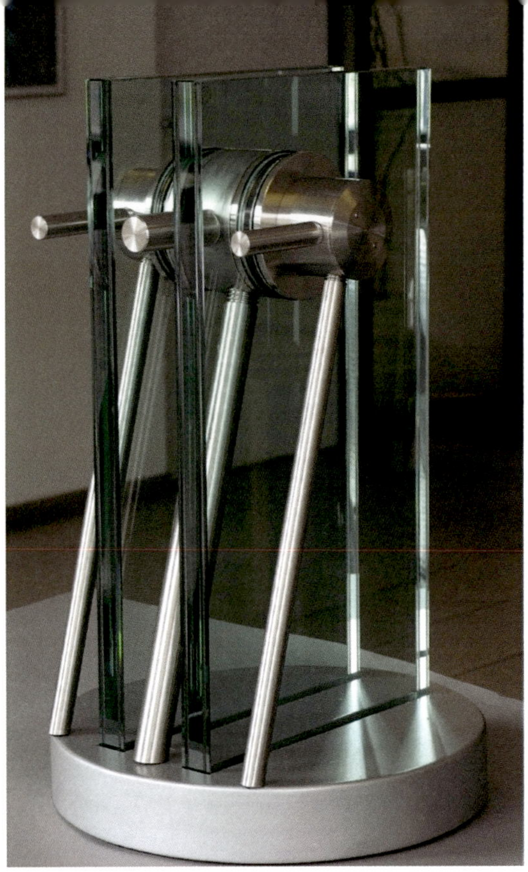

Fig. 102 Principle design of the graduation project of Fokke van Gijn.

He writes: *"However, almost four years after the presentation of this concept we were still discussing and writing letters to lawyers to get the contractor to build it like we wanted it to be built. The contractor was quick to make an alternative proposal to the client; a steel structure with a glass panel cladding. The client and the architect refused. The contractor did not want to build the glass louvres, the name we gave to these glass beams, considering the concept to be unsafe and dangerous, although I wonder whether this point of view is dictated by sheer beneficial interest in the public or by a simple financial calculation. But who am I to say so, having an emotional relationship with the original, unique louvre structure? In 2000 they axed the glass beam. A glittering minimized stainless steel tube with suspension cables now closes the cubic shape of the building. But a lot of valuable knowledge had resulted from this experience".*

In my perspective, the main problem with the Swiss Life louvres was caused by the fairly restricted bearing capacity of glass. Not because of shortcomings in the material, but because of the unavoidable points where the forces have to be transferred to the glass. The existing connections at that time were too weak, unreliable and prone to creep.

Fig. 103 Design for details of a 12 m glass pedestrian bridge and pre-tensioned glued connection by graduation student Fokke van Gijn, now patented. Glass stairs details of Heerema, Leiden which was analyzed and engineered later by engineer Fokke van Gijn.

Fig. 104 Design of a 12 m long pedestrian bridge of graduation student Fokke van Gijn in the model hall of the former Architecture Building at TU Delft, destroyed by fire in 2008.

Eight years after the Swiss Life project, in 2008, Civil Engineering student Fokke van Gijn developed as his graduation thesis in the office of Octatube a new pre-tensioned adhesive connector that coped with inherent problems of these now widely used shear connections. In his proposal the Swiss Life beam could - may be - have been realized. So Swiss Life was 8 years to early!

His pre-tensioned adhesive connection is a reliable and strong glass connection for structural applications. With a lower bound strength of 173 kN, it is 20 times stronger than a standard point fixing for frameless glazing. The glued connection was patented by Octatube, mentioning Fokke van Gijn as the inventor. Besides the high strength, what really sets this connection apart is its behaviour in case of failure. In case that the 19 mm glass panel fails because of overload of the cross-section instead of an unpredictable stress concentration, the glass is just pulled in half. Because of the reliable failure mechanism and the warning before failure by plastic deformation of the stud bolt, which runs through the connection, this is a safe connection.

More than 20 years after completion of the Swiss Life building, the double cable stayed glass beams proposed in vain back then could now be realized, using two main cables as the main structure and a metal mesh laminated in between the PVB films. Or as a beam with the patented glued connections and fully tempered glass. Replacement of a broken glass panel would require extensive scaffolding. It would be a very expensive operation to replace one broken panel in one of the louvers at the costs of at least 50.000,= Euro! Swiss Life was not prepared to insure this risk of breaking glass and its expensive consequences either. One of the last considerations was to have a maintenance apparatus ride over the upper side of the glass panels, which would require a rail, 5 times thicker than the 20 mm cables and stabilizations by the outriggers. As 25 m high cherry pickers do not exist yet, the maintenance would have to be done by a far reaching light crane with a cleaning bucket from an easy accessible position at street level. So this project contained a lot of ambitions without much practical competence or allowance to make a mock-up from which the designers could have learned in the design phase.

Fig. 105 Redesign of the glass louvres of the Swiss Life headquarters by student Fokke van Gijn at Octatube, eight years after completion of the building.

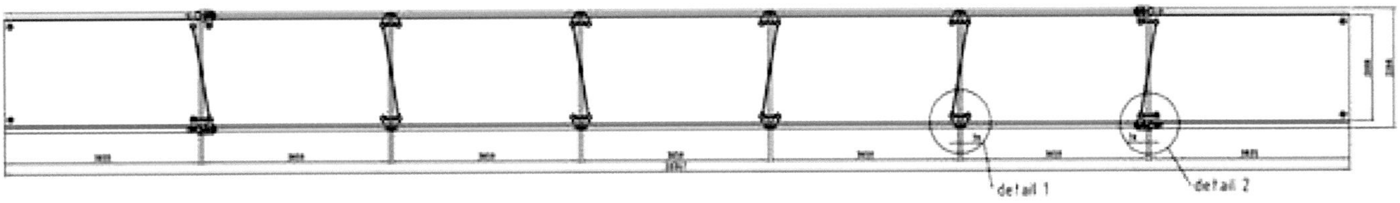

CHAPTER 3.
CONNECTIONS BETWEEN GLASS AND QUATTROS

For centuries panes of glass have been framed by timber windows. The industrial revolution rought metal windows. The increasing quality of industrially produced glass gave rise to larger glass surfaces and an increasing popularity of glass buildings. After World War I the desire for transparent buildings grew. The invention of the float glass production process of annealed glass in the late 1950s enabled Pilkington to introduce flat glass with an accuracy higher than ever before. To date this mid-century invention of float glass making is still the base of the glass industry worldwide. Glass panels can be strengthened thermally, an initiative that became necessary to reduce injuries from the windshields of cars in the 1930s. Even laminated glass dates from that time.

Glass has been known as a material for 5000 years. The production of glass needs high temperatures and therefore much energy. Reduction of fossil energy consumption has become an important issue in the last decades and will be in the coming decades. The sustainable future of the world asks for less energy consumption. Glass has a very high embedded energy through its high temperature of glass melting and further production stages. In the coming decade glass may be regarded as a indurable building material and banned. So efforts will have to be made to bring back the energy consumption of a glass façade in its entire making for example by 50 %, according to a well-published Japanese principle for the car industry [Womack et al, ref 22]. This reasoning is worked out in chapter 7.6.

Glass structures have their own attraction and development. The glass buildings of the 1950s and 1960s were followed by glass fins without any window frames. In 1986, the first large-scale building with frameless glazing was produced in the Serres of the Cité des Sciences et de l'Industrie in La Villette, Paris, designed by RFR. This boosted frameless glazing developments elsewhere, mainly in Western Europe. Amongst architects at that time the development of 'a new building knot' as a symbol of technical architecture was a prestigious task. Much effort went into the design of new connection nodes between glass panels and steel structures. Ever since Konrad Wachsmann wrote his The Turning Point of Building (Wendepunkt im Bauen), 1959 [ref. 20], on the topic of large-scale industrialization of buildings, architects are aware of the complications of the 'building knot'. In those days developing one's own building knot was a feat of technology for an architect. Nowadays we know that the challenges for architects go beyond the knot. Building technology has also to address the demands of sustainability. The baton is now for the digital generation after me.

Opposite page: Fig. 98 Stairs in a royal villa in Jeddah with glass balustrades stabilizing the stairs, design Octatube in collaboration with Atelier One.

Fig. 99 Interior view of Quattro façade at NAI, Rotterdam, 1995, architect Jo Coenen. The connection between the Quattro connectors and the glass was half mechanical / half chemical. Standard system see fig. 142.

Complexity in architecture is much greater than developing a new building node. Complex geometries have been added since, resulting in complex glass nodes. The connection between the glass panels and the load bearing structure in a frameless façade is in principle achieved by point connections. The first connections in the Glass Music Hall in Amsterdam in 1990 were developed as simple glass holes with outside saucers, connecting the glass panel to a spider-like Quattro connector at the inside of the glass by post-stress bolting.

The connector was in turn connected to the metal structure. The glass panels in this project were suspended vertically, so that with the usual safety factor 4 the highest glass panel had to carry a deadweight of 30 kN, which was too much for a normal bolted connection (loaded on shear) in a 8 mm thin glass panel. So a post-stressed bolt connection was used even with sand paper for higher friction between the saucer and the glass. Thanks to the interior situation, this sandpaper was feasible, outside it would degrade fast due to water and frost (fig. 100).

CHAPTER 3.1

Mechanical Connections

The next step after the first single glass connections was to develop connections for double glazing. Usually this was achieved by double holes in both glass panes. This was new for the double glass manufacturers. The air-tightness of the insulated glass panels had to be warranted. Not only of the edges of the glass, which took the industry decades to develop but also holes in the glass panels that came overnight, per project. This was initially done by nylon or POM (polyoxymethylene) circular prop fittings sealed between both panes. This, however, was not easy to achieve and depended very much on production accuracies. The saucers were quite big (50 to 80 mm) and the detail was not suitable for industrial production, but relied on manual production procedures (fig. 101). The glass manufacturers did not give any warrantee. And these connections were rather big and ugly. As none of this was practical, new ideas had to be developed.

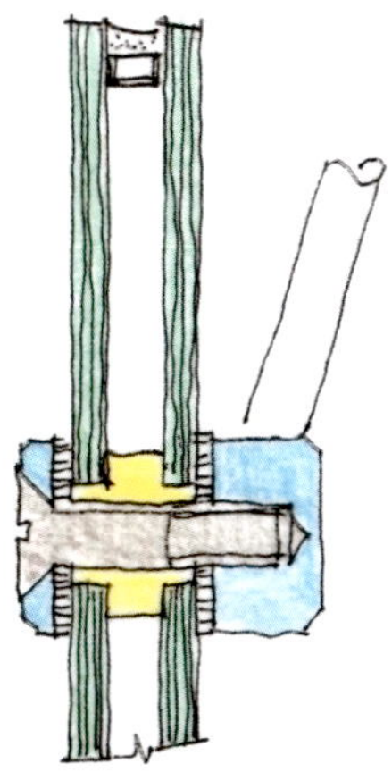

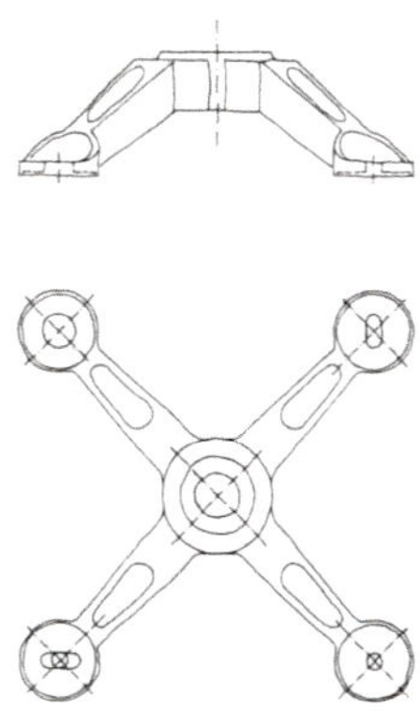

Left: Fig. 100 One of the first Quattro nodes in welded steel for single glass panels in the Glass Music Hall, Amsterdam, 1990.

Middle: Fig. 101 Schematic design for a double perforated glass node with countersunk bolt connected to a Quattro node, 'the big saucer', sketched around 1994, never built.

Right: Fig. 102 Schematic connection design for Finsbury Avenue project, London (architect Sheppard Robson). The node had the dimension of 200 x 200mm.

Figs. 103, 104 Prototype node for modeling purposes (3D printed) and first prototype node, cast in stainless steel, 300 × 300 mm, for the glass cube for Santander Bank, 2008, Madrid.

CHAPTER 3.2

Half Mechanical / Half Chemical Connections

In 1995, we were to develop the connections for the glass façade of the Netherlands Architecture Institute NAI in Rotterdam, architect Jo Coenen. The double glass units were connected in a half mechanical and half chemical mode. The inner pane was drilled and connected by a stainless steel saucer positioned in the air cavity. The outer pane was structurally connected by the sealant between inner and outer pane and water-tightened by the silicone sealant around the perimeter of the double glass panel. The advantages are fewer possible leakage spots and the enabling of a full reflection on the outside. However, the glass suppliers of Octatube would not offer guarantees and workmanship so that Octatube workers had to do the job of connecting the panes in the glass factory in Switzerland. But it proved to be a reliable connection system so that in 2008 the Madrid Glass Cube would get the same connection detailing, see also figure 111,112 and chapter 5.6

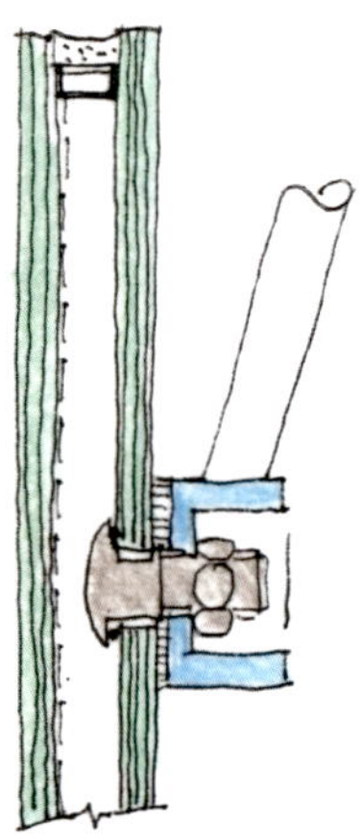

Left: Fig. 105 Half chemical, half mechanical connection in Netherlands Architecture Institute NAI, 1995, Rotterdam, architect Jo Coenen.

Middle: Fig. 106 Sketch of double glass half chemical / half mechanical connection.

Right: Fig. 107 Frameless glass façade around the lobby and the Netherlands Architecture Institute NAI.

Fig. 108, 109 Details of half mechanical / half chemical corner connections in the Santander Glass Cube, 2008, Madrid.

Opposite page:
Fig. 110 Inside view of the Santander Glass Cube with half mechanical / half chemical nodal connections.
Figs. 111, 112 Interior view and exterior views of façade and roof at Santander Glass Cube.

CHAPTER 3.3

Fully Chemical Connections

Fig. 113 Scheme of the fully glued Quattro trumpet connection, with the glue at the inside of the insulated glass panel.

Fig. 114 Fully glued Quattro trumpet connection between inner face of double glass panels and steel loadbearing structure.

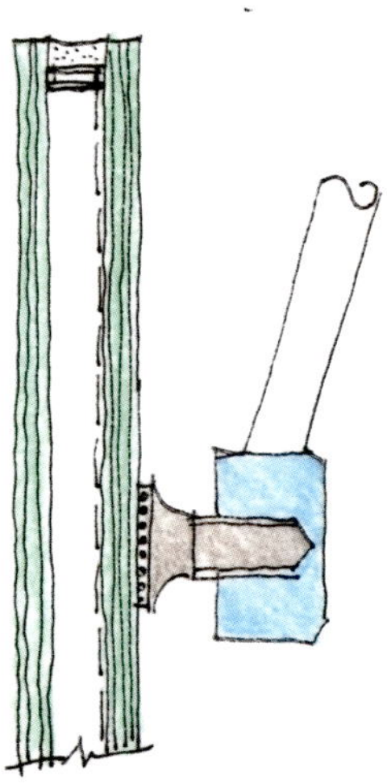

Fig. 115 Sketch of glued Quattro connection seen from outside.

Going from two perforations of the glass pane (fig 101) to one perforation (the solution for Netherlands Architecture Institute NAI, fig 106) was a first experimental step. The next step was obvious to have no perforations at all and to rely on chemical bonding of the internal glass surface to a stainless steel saucer (fig 115). It had been done in 1990 already in the Hulst Flower Shop roof, as an internal (and quite naïve) experiment. Now the experiment involved high-tech glue, selected by the aeronautics-related Gluing Institute at the TU Delft. Tests of selected aeroplane glues were conducted with short-term compression, tension, shear and bending. It was concluded that the compression, tension and shear tests yielded approximately similar results in magnitude (40kN), but that the maximum results of the bending tests only accounted for 10 % of these values. Bending was critical, hence the detailing of the glue connection had to result in minimal bending stresses. Bending had to be prevented at all times. The Flower Shop roof in Hulst (see page 55) had roof panels which were heavy enough to avoid uplift loading. Therefore, the glued connections between double glass panels and Quattro nodes were only loaded in vertical compression.

Fig. 116 Worm eye's view of the Hulst Flower Shop, 1990, architect Walter Lockefeer. For this project, the first fully chemical connections between double glass panels and Quattro nodes were developed.

We developed a standard roof Quattro connection, consisting of stainless steel trumpet connectors which had a 50 mm diameter glue plane on top of the glass while at the mouth of the trumpet a drilled and treated hole was provided into which a single bolt could be screwed, fixing the glued stainless steel connectors to the steel structure.

It proved necessary to machine off the top layer of the glass, as the top layer, though flat to the naked eye, showing a rough surface under the microscope. During the production of double glass units the air in the factory has a high silicone content, which precipitated on the uneven glass surface, filling the valleys. This deposit build-up of silicone on the glass surface causes many glues not to adhere permanently as the silicone doesn't bond with the glue. The same is probably true for many silicone-sealed connections.

The steel trumpet Quattro connector was subjected to both short-term and long-term tests. The glue is applied under high temperature to reduce the curing time to around 8 hours, after which the bonding is tested individually. The steel trumpet connector was patented in a number of European countries and was first applied in 1996 at the roof of the Court of Justice in Maastricht, the Netherlands, and one year later, 1997, in the façade of the Prinsenhof Museum Hall in Delft.

Fig. 117, 118 View from above and below of the first double glass roof with fully glued Quattro nodes at the Court of Justice, Maastricht, architect Gerard Passchier, 1996.

Most of the projects with double and Quattro frameless glazing nowadays involve glued connections. In Germany, special 'Zulassungen im Einzelfall' (specific planning approvals) had to be obtained for this type of connection. The earliest glued nodes installed in 1995 and nowadays are still reliable. There have been no problems with delamination or other forms of failure in the glued connections. Proper treatment of the glass surface is a key to its longevity.

Fig. 119, 120 Exterior and interior glazing on one of the first glass façades with glued connections in Germany at the Fraunhofer Institute, Darmstadt, architect Seidel, Hausmann und Partner, 1998.

If used in a façade, fully glued connections also have deadload to carry and bending moments as its consequence. For that reason, the distance of 50 mm in the trumpet connector detail had to be minimized as much as possible. The trumpet was substituted by a flat stainless steel saucer of 20 mm. Generally speaking a glue connection can transfer compression and tensile forces in the order of 40 kN and shear forces of the same magnitude. However, the experience of the Prinsenhof Museum glass hall in Delft showed that local bending in the nodal glued connection may not exceed 4 kN. The connection detail allows for minimal bending or eccentricity only. In principle, small bending moments will always occur but they have to be analyzed properly.

Fig. 122 Fully glued glass connection details in the façade plane of the Prinsenhof Museum glass hall in Delft, architect Mick Eekhout, 1997.

Fig. 121 Glass façade, office building Lange Voorhout 9, Den Haag, architect Bos & Rosdorff, 1996, with double glass nodes and pre-stressed tensile rods stabilizing the glass panels on both sides. The connections are not bolted, nor glued but clamped from both sides (Arup design).

CHAPTER 4.
THE QUEST FOR 'ZAPPI'

'Zappi' was the name for a transparent and structurally durable hypothetical material yet to be found and developed. The term was coined by Thijs Asselbergs, then the town architect of Haarlem, in an interview just after my appointment as a professor at TU Delft in January 1992. He was a member of 'Booosting' (www.booosting.nl), a group of young architects and industrial designers devoted to industrializing the building industry in The Netherlands since 1988. 'Zappi' was an ideal to work towards, a neverending quest. I also referred to this concept in my inaugural speech at TU Delft in 1992. In the Foreword of this book professor Thijs Asselbergs illuminates his idea behind the word 'Zappi'. It became the collective term for fundamental research at the department of Building Technology of the TU Delft when professor Mick Eekhout was the leading research nestor (2004-2008). The research assessment of the department was excellent.

Broken glass was the most frightful state of glass structures when we started with glass innovations in 1988. Glass breaks when you do not want it to break, Would it also hold when everybody would expect it to break? Where are the borders? How many elephants can a plate of glass carry? How far can we extend the technical border of designing with glass structures of glass compositions?

Back to the chair of Product Development in Architecture and Octatube, back to glass used in structures. The core of the Zappi research was interpreted as the theoretical idea of a stiff, unbreakable glass for structural applications in architecture; the material would be tough, resilient, not prone to sudden breakage and able to deform before yielding. This research took place at the TU Delft, at the chair of Product Development under supervision of Dr. Fred Veer, from 1995 to 2005. Veer, however, immediately pronounced the requested properties as a chemically improbable material combination. While 'Zappi' itself as an in principle unrealistic goal remained out of reach, the research contributed to a number of special projects by Octatube. Architects love to think out of the box and this quest inspired a number of daring solutions. 'Zappi' served for quit a long time as the holy ghost of innovations.

The design & engineering, production & realization of innovative spatial structures with which Mick Eekhout started in 1975, resulted initially in spatial structures of stretched membranes, cable net structures and space frames. And after mid 1980s the material glass which had to cover the slender space structures proved more of a problem and more of a challenge than metal space structures. The dissertation 'Architecture in Space Structures, May 1989' [ref. 16] contained as its very last chapter 'Space Frames and Glass Panels', indicating that the quest for innovation went over from space structures to glass structures. So after 1990 the most of the innovations were executed in glass structures instead

Opposite page: Fig. 123 Fully glued glass connection details in the roof plane and façade of the Prinsenhof Museum glass hall in Delft, architect Mick Eekhout, 1997.

of spatial structures. This entire book is devoted to the results of this 'Quest for Zappi' of the incremental innovative approach of glass structures in the Octatube company.

SOLUTIONS INSPIRED BY ZAPPI

One of those daring designs was a structural glass staircase (see page 68). Atelier One from London invited us in 1995 to engineer and build a staircase and interior façades in a royal villa in Jeddah. The design axiom of a 3D spirally deformed steel tube was chosen on the base of which the glass stairs would be cantilevered. But since users normally walk on the outer side, where the treads are widest, the treads have to be balanced. This need is met by the glass balustrade which therefore had to be continuous and have a firm connection at the ground level and at the first floor level, at the height of 5 m. The continuously hot-bent balustrade panels are connected to the stair treads and to the baluster tube by bolting and are continuous in form. The deformation of the 3D bent steel spine was by no means perfect, so the elliptical cross section was one problem but the deviations from the theoretical spiral were more severe. Hence the cantilevering rods that support the stair treads had to be dimensioned in the factory and the entire staircase had to be prefabricated. After assembly in the villa, the glass panels in the balustrade were loaded in shear and stabilized the stairs. The adjacent glass partitioning interior façades of this villa contained switchable glass. The owner asked the designers after the installation of the staircase whether it would be possible to change the flat laminated stair elements also in the similar switchable glass as well, just for the pleasure of being the first in the world.

Fig. 124, 125 Glass stairs in Jeddah, Atelier One, 1998, with structural glass balustrade. Left as a design, right after realization.

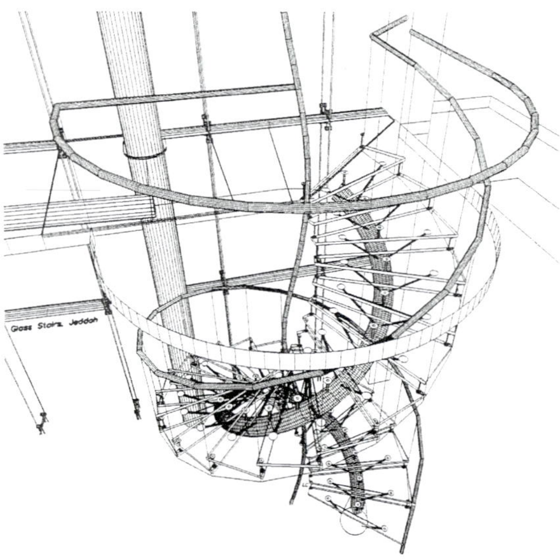

CHAPTER 4.1

Glass Compression Tubes

An exciting new technology was explored by graduation student Joost Pastunnik in 1998. He conducted compression tests on laminated tubes of borosilicate laboratory glass. The inner glass tube was loaded with compression. The outer tube was a little shorter, not loaded in compression and acting as the fracture safety shield of the inner tube. The space between both tubes was filled by clear acrylic resin. Due to the shrinkage during curing it appeared that the interspace between two tubes was hard to fill with acrylic in longer pieces. A proper production discipline was yet missing. So this lamination required some more ingenuity. From the tests it appeared that even fully broken tubes could resist a compression force of 110 kN. They would break and buckle around 120 kN. This would mean that a roof surface of 10 × 10 m2 could be supported by a single glass column! We assumed that a breakthrough in the safe use of structural glass elements loaded in compression was imminent and expected a phase of up-scaling of the columns to real building size to follow. We negotiated with Schott on the base of the patent that had been granted, but in vain. It was a few years later that we learned that Schott found another partner in Germany to further develop this technology in the person of Stefan Behling, from 1995 until 2015 head of the building construction department at Stuttgart University. In 2003, architect Norman Foster realized the office building Tower Park', near the Tower of London, using laminated glass compression members. The problem of shrinking acrylic was overcome by film-laminating two half cylinders of glass outside the central glass tube.

Fig. 126 Broken but still functioning glass compression bar at the Tower Park office building in London, architect Norman Foster, 2003.

Fig. 127 Glass tube compression test by graduation student Joost Pastunnik. The broken inner tube still takes 110 kN of compression force, thanks to the protecting outer tube.

Fig. 128 Prototype of tension stabilized compression stud in solid glass with a 40 mm diameter, designed by Octatube, 2000.

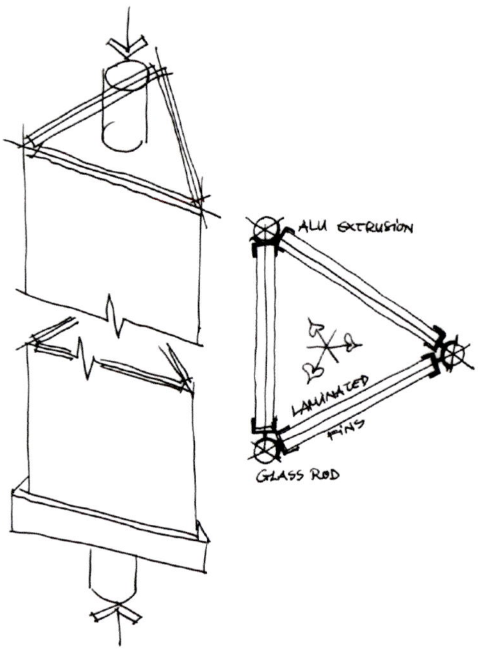

Fig 129 Design sketch of triangular glass column composed of two to five blades of laminated and fully tempered glass, in which the corners stabilize the fins.

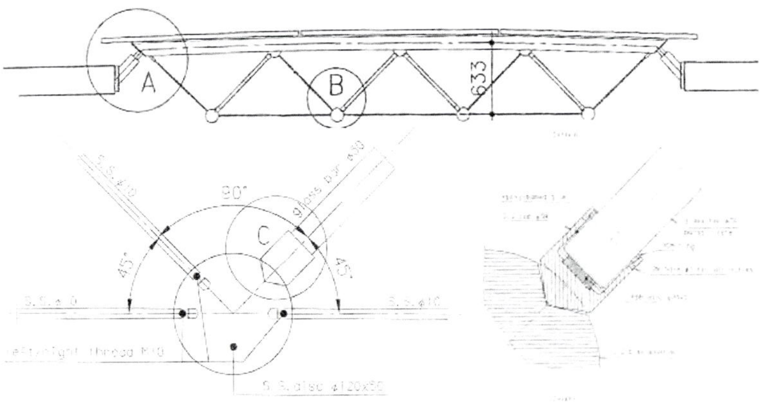

Fig. 130 Details of glass stud for Swiss Life roof in Amstelveen after principle design of Rob Nijsse and detail engineering of Octatube, architect Pi de Bruijn, 1997.

Fig. 131 Bottom: built result

During a visit to Tower Park in summer 2010, we noticed four broken glass cylinders with breaking patterns typically for borosilicate glass. Yet the glass bars functioned without a problem, testifying the merits of this technology.

The first application of glass studs happened in trusses in the Amstelveen headquarters of Swiss Life (see page 63). Structural engineer Rob Nijsse of ABT had made a design with glass compression studs, which we engineered as solid bars, with stainless steel caps ending in a central point to avoid any bending in the connection and in the shaft. These glass studs were now 3 m long so that it was necessary to prevent their buckling by an external stabilizing system. Glass studs were also applied in two glass canopies at Schiphol Airport, Amsterdam. In this case the 30 mm diameter solid glass rods were stabilized against buckling by three steel rod stabilizers.

GLASS COMPRESSION STUDS FOR OVERHEAD STRUCTURES

Chinese research fellow Dr. Li Zang participated in the research on glass bars in 2001 in the TU Delft under supervision of Prof. Dr. Jaap Wardenier and the author. She analyzed the behaviour of glass compression studs compared to steel compression studs in a number of different 'tensegrity' arrangements: diagonal, orthogonal, radial. The theoretical outcome of her research was that glass studs were as reliable as steel studs. In 2004, vertical glass studs were used in the 30 m diameter roof at Bancopolis Madrid, architect Kevin Roche (see pages 101, 102).

Fig. 132 Canopy at Schiphol office building, Amsterdam, architect Nefkens, 2000.

Fig. 133 Canopy at Schiphol office building, detail of glass compression bar as realized by Octatube.

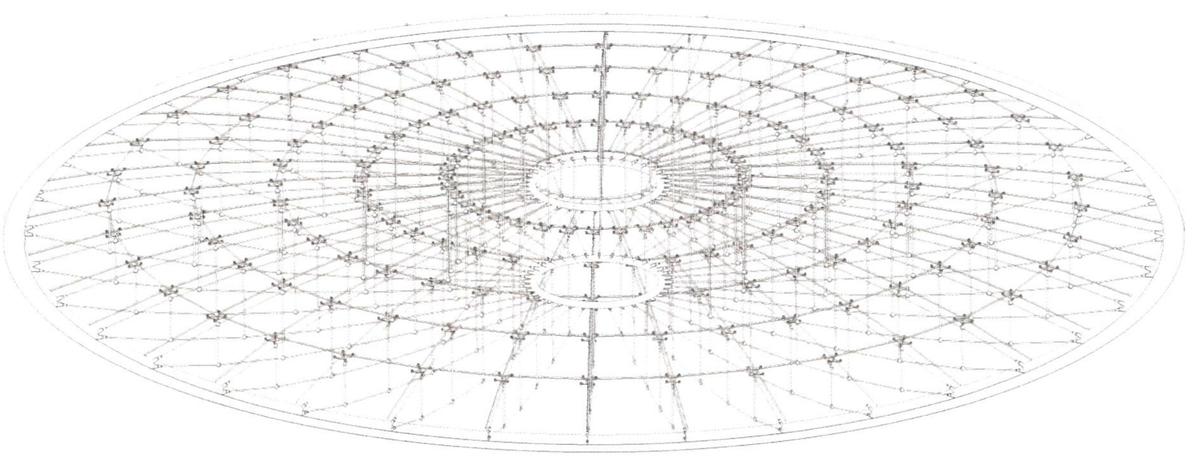

Fig. 134 Octatube proposal of 30 m circular roof with vertical glass studs for Bancopolis Madrid for architect Kevin Roche, 2004.

CHAPTER 4.2

Overcladding of Existing Facades

The double glass façade for the Deutsche Bank/Guggenheim Museum at Unter den Linden in Berlin was designed by architects Novotny Mähner Assoziierte in order to create a transition between the existing stone façade and the new double steel and aluminium layer characterized by its play of reflection.

Fig. 135, 136 Façade and details of Deutsche Bank/ Guggenheim Museum at Unter den Linden, Berlin, architect Novotny Mähner Assoziierte, 1997.

The glazing was monolithic clear fully tempered glass with stainless steel frames that acted as projections of the existing window scheme. We found out that the substantial building tolerances of this 200-years-old building made by hand had led to ingenious detailing to achieve a uniform appearance. Generally speaking repetition in old buildings is the result of handicraft and has large tolerances. Only since industrialization one can speak of tolerances in expected ranges. It is known that Henry Ford only invented the assembly line in 1908 after he developed a production discipline to avoid 'plus-tolerances' at all costs. Only 'minus-tolerances' were allowed. From then on all elements and components fitted into each other and did not have to be worked on or machined by hand in an atelier. Old buildings usually date to an era prior to this development.

A few years later the necessity of upgrading an office building in Germany provided another opportunity for installing an overcladding. The client was the Sparkasse of Ludwigshafen. The bank occupied an office tower in the centre of Ludwigshafen, built in the 1980s style of exposed concrete. The windows were not well insulated thermally. So the plan was to achieve the necessary energetic upgrading by installing a second skin around the building. The profile of the building would remain apparent, but the glass cladding would give it a distinctly different character. Dr. Thiemo Ebbert used the upgrading of this office tower in his PhD study 'Re-face, Refurbishment Strategies for the Technical Improvements of Office Façades' , 2010, [ref.30].

The XXX-system designed in collaboration with a development group in Langen, Germany, led by Rolf Evers, comprises the enwrapping with a new glass façade around existing office buildings to improve the thermal and acoustic performance of the skin, to individualize the ventilation, heating and cooling while the office spaces could be occupied and fully used. This design concept is especially suited for the technical renovation of 30–40 years old inner city buildings: the glass sound screen can give old stucco buildings a fresh outlook and can even be provided with a graphical design. The acoustical function of the screen is not spoiled by the flow of fresh air through the skin.

Fig. 137, 138 Original view of Sparkasse Ludwigshafen, Germany, and view after installation of a second skin façade, Sander Hofrichter Architekten, 2002, in collaboration with PhD student Thiemo Ebbert, Ulrich Knaack, Rolf Evers and others.

Middle: Fig. 139, 140 Existing office tower and redesign of façade in the Voorhof, Delft, architect Walter Lockefeer, 2010.

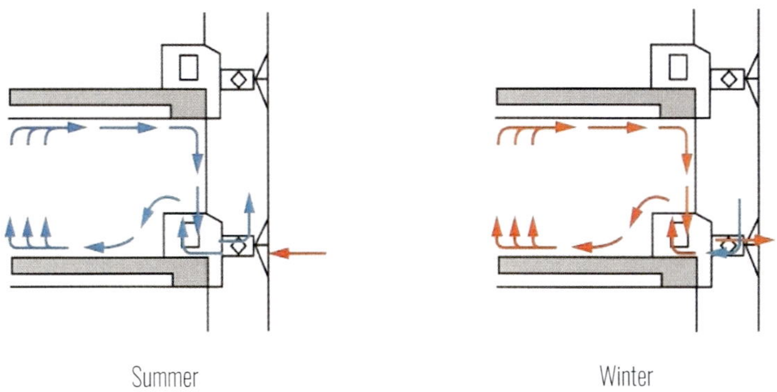

Bottom: Fig. 141 Double façade proposals for cooling and heating with equipment outside the existing skin in the so called 'XXX-system' in summer and winter conditions.

CHAPTER 5.
SUPER-SLENDER SUPPORTING STEEL STRUCTURES

One of the principles of the Octatube design & build company was the possibility to design structures with a high degree of refinement, both in system and in detail. We developed systems that followed bending moment lines. Thus the bending moment lines were visualized. Working with pure tension in cables or tensile rods made the structural action very clear, resulting in an intelligent material appearance. These structures are set up with the simple knowledge of bending moment lines from equally distributed wind loadings, which essentially are catenary lines in the geometrical sense. But wind is dynamic and does not have in reality an equal distribution of forces. For that reason it would be good practice to anticipate fluctuations in wind pressures on the façades. The realized constructions have to contain triangulations or cross elements to allow for asymmetrical wind loadings. The glass panels have hinged lines at each side line. The flexibility in form is accommodated by the hinging heads of the Quattro nodes, so the corner deformations of the glass panels are important. In reality the deformation of the glass panels is also a function of the thickness of the glass panels versus the span between the supporting nodes. In many flat roof applications, the tensile forces cannot be obtained from the existing adjacent buildings around the glass façade or glass roofs. In those cases, additional compression tubes in the roof construction are introduced independent of the existing loadbearing structure.

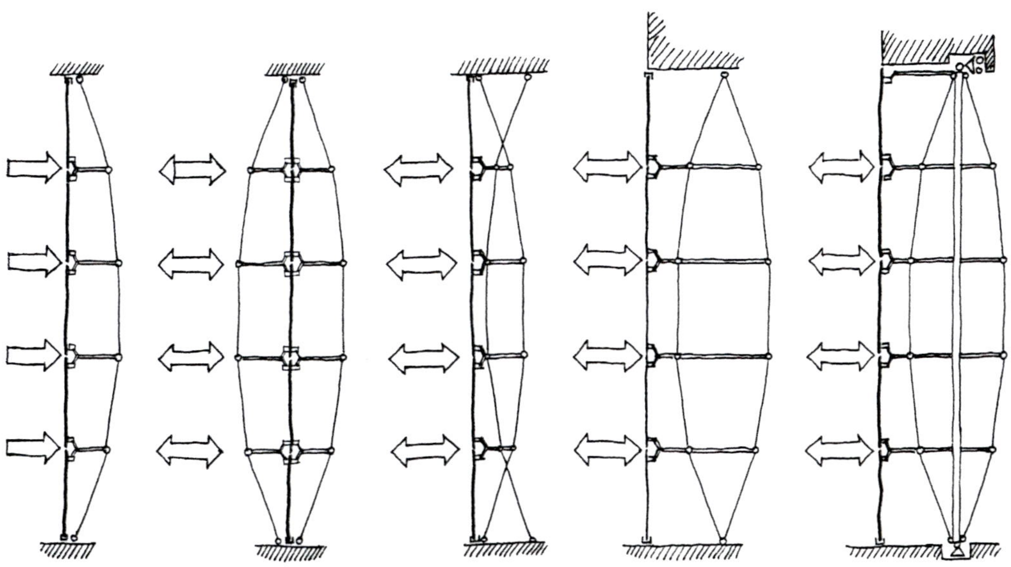

Fig. 143 Several structural schemes of vertical open cable systems for glass façades. The right hand schemes are closed systems in which the compression is in balance with tension.

Opposite page: Fig. 142 nterior view of the glass façade of the OZ Building in Tel Aviv, 16 m wide and 52 m high, architect Avram Yaski, 1991.

CHAPTER 5.1

All Tensile Structures

Fig. 144 Exterior view of the OZ Building façade in Tel Aviv, Avram Yaski, 1991.

Fig. 145 Interior view of the OZ Building façade in Tel Aviv with its extremely slender stabilizing tensile structure.

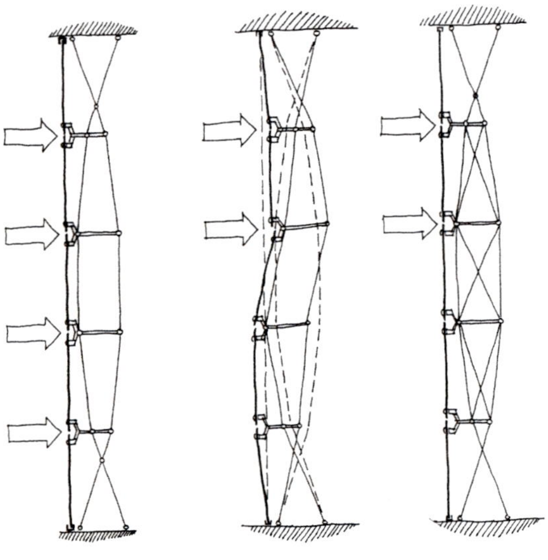

Fig. 146 Principle schemes of internal structural triangulation of the ultra slender tensile trusses of the OZ Building façade in Tel Aviv.

An example of an all-tensile lightweight structure is the fishbone-shaped tensile construction with solid tensile rods, as realized in the OZ Building in Tel Aviv, in collaboration with architect Avram Yaski, 1991. The system consisted of horizontal tensile trusses each 3.6 m at floor heights for easy connection to horizontal reaction forces from the floors and a secondary system of vertical stabilizers at the intermediate points 1.8 m distances. This weave of horizontal and vertical tensile trusses was completed by straight vertical deadweight suspenders, leading the complete deadweight of the glass façade up to the roof structure of the building. The height of the façade was 52 m; the span in horizontal direction 16 m. The glass panels were laminated 6.6.2 mm clear and fully tempered glass panels. Both maintenance and possible replacing of glass is handled from a suspended cradle from the roof. In 20 years of service not a single panel ever broke. The façade has a northern orientation. Later information from the Centre of Desert Research in Beer Sheva corrected the assumption that the north orientation would avoid solar radiation. Thanks to the dust and desert particles in the air the indirect solar radiation on this north façade is almost as much as any other façade orientations.

Opposite page: Fig. 147 Hand sketch of the OZ Building geometry of tensile trusses.

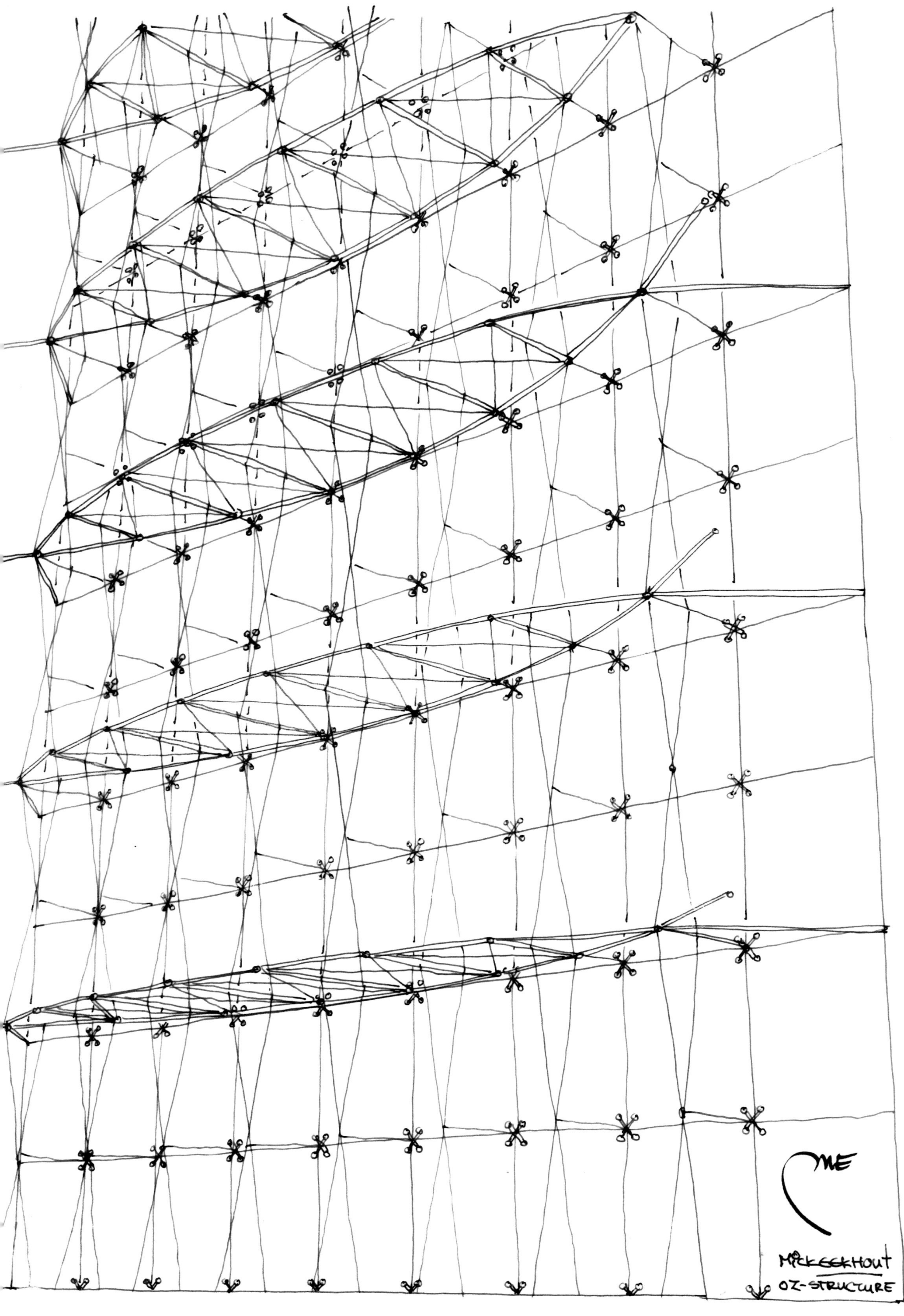
ME
MICK EEKHOUT
OZ-STRUCTURE

In the last two decades a remarkable rise in wind loadings has been experienced. In the interior Amsterdam Glass Music Hall of 1990 0.3 kN/m2 had been calculated; normal wind forces are around 1.0 kN/m2 as at the OZ Building, but an extreme value was 5.25 kN/m2 wind loading at the Citibank Plaza in Hong Kong. We had to make sure that the tensile trusses could absorb the compression and suction forces from the wind load; the trusses form a catenary line both inward and outward, loaded in tension only.

The façade, which had to deal with very high wind loads, consists of frameless glazing with tensile trusses. The trusses would receive the compression and suction loadings on the façade and turn them into minimal tensile forces.

Fig. 148 Exterior of Citibank Plaza in Hong Kong, architect Rocco Yim, 1993.

In Hong Kong, a tower for Citibank, designed by architect Rocco Yim, next to I. M. Pei's bank of China, was developed in 1992 and had to be built the year after. To make sure that the tower would be completed well before the takeover of Hong Kong by the republic of China in 1997 (and its expected economic slump), it had to be built with the enormous velocity of one floor per day. So the building was built during day and night. partly built at night. The scaffolding was – as it is customary in Hong Kong – made of bamboo, 250 m high. The entrance lobby was to be day-lit by 32 m high façades, which were to be as transparent as possible. But at the same time the US client, following the American façade specifications, called for a typhoon loading and a mock-up to prove the developed façade system would work. So even this typhoon wind loading of 5.25 kN/m2 was answered by a system mostly the same as developed for the OZ Building. First the deadweight and the wind loadings were separated. The horizontal spans were 10 m and 12 m, while the height was 32 m. Logically the wind span would be horizontal: the shortest track of 10–12 m times the 5.25kN/m2 loading. It resulted in a catenary set of double tensile elements of 24 mm diameter. They were doubled in order to cope with relative slender tensile elements, nodes and turnbuckles.

The rod material was stainless steel. The 'Quattro' connectors were welded in mild steel. After completion of the first ten floors of the lower concrete work, the façade opening was measured and, because of the day-and-night cycle of the concrete work, large deviations from the theoretical lines were measured, up to 100 mm on either side. So the decision was taken to cut a 100 mm sleeve into the concrete walls bordering the façades and to shorten and elongate the tensile elements in turnbuckles. That allowed prefabrication of the elements in the Netherlands and installation in Hong Kong with large adjustments.

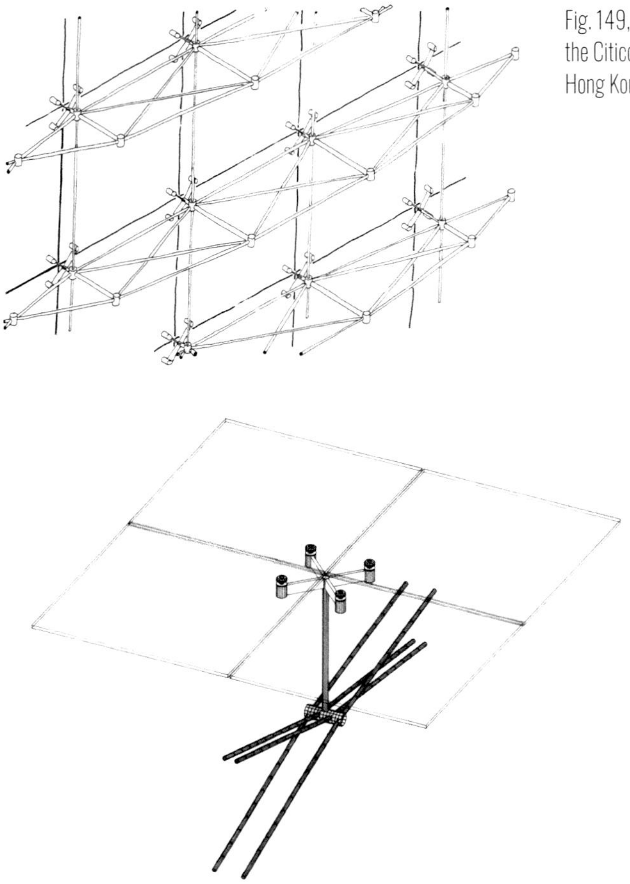

Fig. 149, 150 Details of the Citicorp façades in Hong Kong, 1993.

The specifications asked for an extensive wind test as it is customary in the US. At TNO, The Netherlands Organisation for applied scientific research, in Delft, in 1992 a closed test box was made in which three horizontal trusses were installed with glass panels. The box had to be watertight and windtight to ensure constant air pressure. In the box overpressure and underpressure was generated by means of a static air-compressor. Outside two giant wind ventilators were installed that produced dynamic wind pressure and suction. The loading was assumed as a 1.0 kN/m2 plus and minus cycle, then a 1.5 kN cycle, a 2.0 kN cycle and so on. All parties were present: the Hong Kong client, the Hong Kong architect, the Hong Kong structural engineer, the US façade advisor, the Japanese glass manufacturer, the Hong Kong façade installer, the Delft Octatube crew and the Delft TNO installation and testing crew. During the cycles with loads above 4.0 kN the glass panels started to bend outward and inward in a frightening mode. In the 5.0 kN cycle two panels exploded suddenly and the glass particles were shattered outward in the laboratory grounds over a distance of 20 m. The test had failed and all were shocked.

Octatube investigated the structural system. The Japanese glass supplier, Central Glass, checked the glass panels. Of course the architect and the client had doubts. All elements were carefully examined and, after the first shock was over, the cause was found in the downward sagging of the trusses where the glass panels disappeared too deep in the lower U-channel. For the same reason the highest panels did not have enough overlap to allow for the bulging out of the glass panels during high pressures. The upper glass panels shortened too much for the upper U-channel, sprang out of channel and by the sheer force of the overpressure exploded into fragments. That was not without danger as the 15 mm thick fully pre-stressed glass panels were laminated by 3 mm float glass for safety reasons. This float glass appeared to be more vulnerable than the 15mm glass panel it had to protect. The problem was a simple installation problem caused by too much haste.

Fig. 151 Interior of the Citicorp façades in Hong Kong.

In the book Skyskraper: The Making of a Building by Karl Sabbagh [ref. 23], the story of the design, development, production and on-site building of the One Worldwide Plaza skyscraper in New York is told. In it, there is a remarkable chapter on prototype testing, which was quite parallel to our experiences. The top of the skyscraper had to be tested in a mock-up.

This mock-up had more conventional materials, but had been done in too short a time for the silicone to cure properly. In addition to that, not the correct materials were used and other small deviations from plan were built into the mock-up. The result was a failure of the wind and water penetration test at the famous Construction Research Laboratory in Miami, Florida, one of world's foremost testing facility for curtain walls. The book explains on 30 pages why this went wrong. One has to take one's time in building the mock-up. The testing of the second mock-up went smoothly and is treated in the book only by a short description. We learn more from our failures than from our successes. The second test in Delft with more precision and more checks during the assembly went flawlessly and the approval for production was given immediately. The actual glass panels were installed as 15 mm monolithic glass panels, fully pre-stressed. Today, the two glass façades have been in place for almost 30 years and only need regular cleaning of the glass and the metal elements.

CHAPTER 5.2

Earthquake-Resistant Quattro Node Systems

For a furniture shop in Mexico City I was approached by an industrial designer who called from New York when he had the book about the Glass Music Hall of Amsterdam in his hands. ref 15]. The result was a project in Mexico City with glass facades, fully crossed out with diagonal tie rods and Quattro nodes at a distance of 1.5 m that remained completely rigid during earthquakes. The concrete wall next to it, 9 m high, had a deformation during earthquakes of 300 mm horizontally on top, so we had to keep away from that wall with a 300 mm rubber flap. The Quattro glass facades were rigid.

Fig. 152 Front of three storey furniture shop 'Moda in Casa' in Mexico City, architect Enrico Norten, 1996 in frameless Quattro glazing. This façade was made in Quattro glazing where each glass panel was diagonally stabilized by tensile wind bracings. It survived all later earthquakes in Mexico City after the disastrous Big Quake of 1985.

Up until 1993, all façade and roof constructions were designed and developed to absorb loadings perpendicular to the surface (wind and snow loads and the deadweight of the roof) and sometimes static loads (i.e. deadweight) in plane of the façades, but never dynamic loads from that direction. Central Glass of Japan, the glass supplier for the Citibank Plaza in Hong Kong, wanted to develop the Quattro node system for the Japanese market. It had proven itself under the local high typhoon wind loadings but the question was whether the static node system could be adapted to accommodate seismic movements of the loadbearing structure, specifically for tall buildings? Central Glass, recovered from the failure of the first prototype test at TNO Delft, was eager enough to learn about Octatube's expertise. And they requested further development of the regular Quattro node system into a seismically resistant Quattro SR system, suitable for the Japanese market.

The relatively simple welded Quattro nodes had to be changed into a more dynamic connection, allowing lateral movement. After extensive studies this led to a new concept of the Quattro joint. The earthquake loading on a building can be absorbed quite easily if the movements are vertical. If the stresses are horizontal, however, in particular a tall building will sway horizontally. So the problem was how to accommodate lateral movement of the glass panel, caused by swaying of the building in the plane of the glass. For fully glazed façades with dot point connections of Quattro nodes the perpendicular movement of the façade plane was not so much the problem as all joints would behave like hinges. But the lateral movement would be extremely critical. A tall building under horizontal earthquake loading, completely glazed in this design exercise, would cause the glass façade to be moving in its horizontal rows of glass panels.

The idea was to have the panels move freely in horizontal rows or bands and to facilitate the sliding of the two upper dot point connections at the two upper panel corners in relation to the two lower dot points. In the centre of the Quattro joint a sliding mechanism was provided. The joint was now composed of an upper half of two connection ears and a lower half of two connection ears with an intermediate sliding mechanism. How to ensure that the outward movement after the earthquake would cause the panel rows to return to their original position?

Fig. 153 The mock-up test rig for frameless glazing with earthquake-resistant Quattro SR nodes at Central Glass company in Tokyo, 1994 (note the samurai corners).

The solution to this problem was designed as a double hinge, which would be able to allow for the horizontal movement and, by virtue of the elongation of the sideward angles during movement a sort of spring action would result, which would press the two Quattro node halves again into the original position. All these movements would have to accounted for, knowing that the tolerances from production were extremely small, within 1 mm. The vertical silicone seams were executed with standard silicone sealant, but the sealant of the horizontal seams had a much larger deformability, more than 200 %. With this the mechanism, the movement of the concrete skeleton could be followed during earthquakes without loss of watertightness or airtightness. Just like many other Japanese companies, Central Glass followed an extensive process of research before the definitive Quattro SR system joints were tested.

A specially designed and engineered test rig was built for this system, consisting of a rather heavy exterior frame with an airtight steel overpressure/underpressure chamber behind it of 10 × 10 m and 3 m deep, with an inner frame of two vertical and two horizontal members, connected with four hinging corners. The test rig had been detailed with corner reinforcements on the outer frame reminiscent of a samurai sword. The inner frame could be moved by hydraulic action as far as 120 mm sideward, thus simulating seismic deformation. This was the deformation calculated for three vertical panels connected by two rows of Quattro SR nodes. The Quattro SR connection was developed by going through a series of four different approaches, from a large to a rather concentrated model, but in line with the concept of horizontal rows of glass panels and sliding movement in between the panels.

All tests were carried out successfully. The glass used was 20 mm fully tempered glass laminated with 3 mm float glass on the inside for safety reasons. Again, no panel broke and the 3 mm safety glass pane was more vulnerable to breakage that the 20 mm panels. The first application of the Quattro node façades were at the Seiroko hospital complex in Tokyo was developed shortly afterwards and installed in 1993. Central Glass later informed us that an earthquake at the Richter scale 6 had occurred with no damage whatsoever to the façade. The patent obtained for the system went to Central Glass for Japan and to Octatube for the rest of the world.

Fig. 154 Quattro node tests of the mock-up test rig at Central Glass company in Tokyo.

Fig. 155 The Quattro SR double-hinged node able to accommodate horizontal movement of the rows of frameless glass panels.

Fig. 156 Mick Eekhout showing the Quattro SR node with double hinges to allow large horizontal movement between horizontal rows of glass panels.

CHAPTER 5.3
Fish Bone Structures

Many applications of frameless glazing for roofs are designed for existing buildings and some of them even for older listed buildings. However, relying on reaction forces from the existing building itself is usually impossible. So these glass structures on top of monuments have to be self-supporting, i.e. autonomous from the building's loadbearing structure and foundations. This is the reason why super-slender tensile trusses (without compression elements integrated) as described before cannot be used in monuments, as they require large reaction forces and brickwork buildings fail to produce additional forces in tension, compression and bending. Therefore, the necessary compression forces must be provided otherwise. If tensile trusses are arranged in a lens-form, dictated by bending moment lines, it is possible to introduce a central compression steel tube, so that in all cases of downward and upward loading the tensile truss with central tube acts as an independent beam, yet maintaining its elegance. These 'bow-

Fig. 157 Interior view of the Prinsenhof Museum glass hall, also known as the 'Van der Mandele Hall', with its slender steel structure, frameless glazing, acoustic baffles and the view out to the historic Wallonian Curch, (Waalse Kerk).

string' trusses are composed of a central compression tube, an upper tension cable and a lower tension cable, connected regularly by outrigging compression studs. The double bow string truss for the glass hall in the Prinsenhof Museum of Delft follows this principle.

Its trusses are spaced at 2.5 m centres to accommodate the covering double glass units of 2.5 m. The glass panels were composed as extremely light packages of double glass, due to budget reasons: 8 mm on top and 5.5.2 on bottom. The panels are supported at 1/5th from the corners. They have a very minimal thickness to the span and they were barely stiff enough to allow for application of the sealant. The deer horn model of supports was derived from a maximal lightweight use of glass. Total thickness was 18 mm only.

In the positioning of the columns spaced at 5 m centres and the trusses spaced every 2.5 m, a regular support system was fixed for the glass panels, sized 1.8 x 2.5 m. In order to support these slender double glass panels, the top members of the trusses were provided with 'deer horn' glass supports, with 1 m width. Glass supports were spaced at 1.6 x 2.0 m. The top glass panels were 8 mm and the lower panels 5.5.1 mm were extremely light.

The connections between glass panels and duo supports were glued. During the installation it turned out that the silicone

Fig. 158 The glass hall of the Prinsenhof Museum during the yearly summer Chamber Music Festival which has been taking place here since 1997.

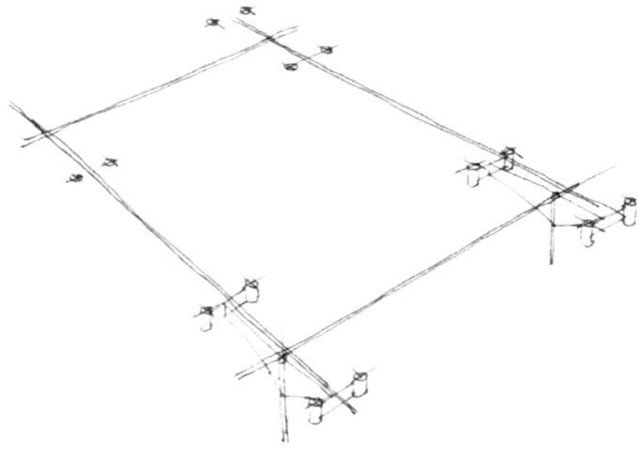

Fig. 159 Scheme of the 'deer horn' supports @ 5 m centres, enabling the use of extremely thin glass: 5+16+5.5 mm fully tempered glass.

sealers needed sliding working platforms of plywood with foam to kneel on and do their work. The glass panels were quite sensitive to asymmetrical loading as exerted by a person standing or kneeling on the outer edge of the glass panels. A cantilevering glass panel bends when one stands on the outer tip and the other panel is then not loaded and not deformed. Today's practice would be to work with thicker glass panels and make a span of 2.5 m right from the beginning, but the careful and minimalized use of materials back in 1996 called for a different approach.

The stabilization of the entire hall had to be attained. The roof structure was clamped between the existing brick buildings and only the gable end opposite

Fig. 160 Glass roof for the Westelijk Handelsterrein at Van Vollenhovenstraat in Rotterdam, architect Jan van der Weerd, 2001.

the Waalse Kerk (Wallonian Chapel) could swing sideward. This led to a diagonal bracing of the façade, with a central elliptical steel column as the compression element. In the gable façade the spatial stabilization of the square spider web was used not only to stabilize the façade in lateral direction, but also to connect the Quattro connectors on studs from the glass panel corners to the four corners of the steel structure, so that in the field only tensile forces would function and the tensile elements could be dimensioned very slender. The view of the Waalse Kerk was disturbed only minimally.
The acoustics were another consideration. The shallow, cylindrical form of the roof would result in bad acoustics as all reflections would concentrate in a central line. However, the space was so romantic that only four months after opening the idea arose to organize a summer festival of chamber music. For that reason suspended acoustical buffers were installed, designed by Kees Spanjers and with Rob Metkemeijer as acoustical advisor.

Five years later the roof over the café street of the Westelijk Handelsterrein at the Van Vollenhovenstraat in Rotterdam was designed for architect Jan van de Weerd. The trusses, resembling a ‘flying kite’, were spaced at the same distance as the existing brickwork walls perpendicular to the street walls for stability reasons. On top of the trusses and perpendicular above them a system of elliptical tubes was installed to which the glass panels were fixed. The glass panels were also regarded to carry over shear forces because of wind: there are no steel wind bracings. The roof has two open ends and sidewards a 100 mm high ventilation space was kept, enough to satisfy the fire-prevention authorities. The steel tubes have a slightly

arched form to emphasize the 'flying kite' character of the glass roof. These tubes are the compression studs connected with an upwards and a downwards tensile rod, forming together the stability system for uplift and downwards loadings. As the street covering is only meant to prolong the summer season, both into spring as well as into autumn, laminated fully pre-stressed glass was used. The use of small elliptical CHS profiles gave the roof a smooth and abstract character. The glass is laid on the ellipses and is held by upside down U-profiles. This application can be seen as a simpler version of the façade construction at the Prinsenhof Museum but under less demanding circumstances. The historic synagogue of the Liberal Jewish Community in The Hague, the so-called Portuguese 'Snoge', was built in the middle of the 18th century and is a classicist architectural monument. It even survived the Second World War. The synagogue complex needed an extension between the street front 'gracht' house and the hidden synagogue in the backyard with a glass hall for social gatherings and festivities. Mick Eekhout was invited as the architect and designed a cubical glass construction with an apex almost as high as the existing synagogue. The tubular structure is covered with a glass roof and has four glass façades. The roof is supported by four free-standing legs on the ground floor level which are connected to the existing walls. The glass cube frames the front part of the synagogue, thus highlighting it with respect.
In the Hague it is not allowed to cover the back yards between street buildings and garden buildings. The client was therefore careful enough to have the architect design different alternative coverings.

Fig. 161 Design of Glass Hall at the Portuguese Synagogue in The Hague, embracing the classical monument from 1753 with a modern classic glass hall,, architect Mick Eekhout, 2004.

Fig. 162 Glass Hall, Portuguese Synagogue, The Hague. Axonometric drawing of the roof construction.

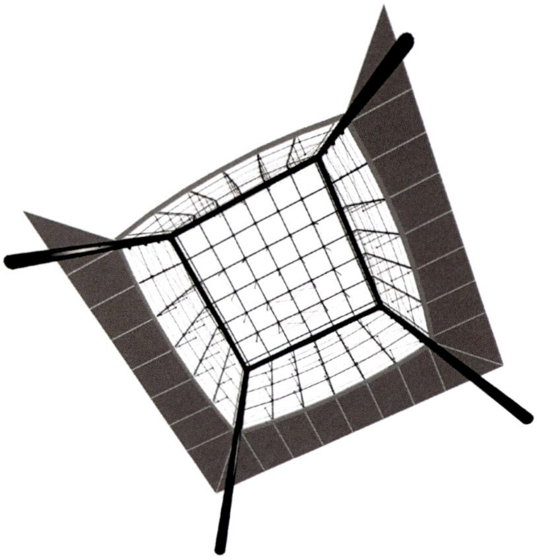

When the Jewish Community discussed the project with mayor Wim Deetman, they were allowed to cover the entire backyard as a compensation of sufferings from World War II, since it had been promised to them in the past. The most prominent design alternative was chosen, twice the costs of the others. It took two more years to collect the necessary funds, but thanks to the mayor this alternative was realized. The steel frame was given an infill of four slightly curved glass façades and a glass roof with a gutter in line of the cube, allowing for minimal glass edges on top.

Fig. 163 View of the suspended glass roof of the Glass Hall at the Synagogue from below.

For the glass panels, green body tinted glass was chosen, fully tempered and laminated on the inside. The central panels in the roof can be opened, more out of religious reasons for instance at 'Sukkoth' or Feasts of Tabernacles) than ventilation. The metal panels are perforated, leading to excellent acoustics, advised by Rob Metkemeijer. This Glass Hall is perfect for chamber music and for lectures, even without a microphone.

Fig. 164 The Glass Hall at the Portuguese Synagogue is frequently used for all kind of social gatherings and receptions. Lectures – here by Bill Gates – can be delivered without a microphone, thanks to the good acoustics of the space achieved by sound-absorbing metal panels.

CHAPTER 5.4

A Circular 'Flying Saucer' Roof

For a 30 m diameter circular roof, designed for the New York architect Kevin Roche (1922–2019, who took over Eero Saarinen's office and was awarded the Pritzker Prize in 1982) for the main building at Santander Group City near Madrid, a radial arrangement of tensile trusses was developed, surrounded by a steel ring of RHS 350 × 350 mm. The upper and lower rods were to be 30 mm and post-stressed for the required stiffness. The vertical elements were executed in stainless steel as well, although an alternative in glass bars had been investigated. Research fellow Li Zhang had worked for one year on the comparison between glass and steel compression studs in these types of tensegrity arrangements and concluded that glass tubes were perfectly trustworthy structural components. The proposals for the architect were therefore submitted in two versions, steel studs and glass studs. Our competitor was the Barcelona-based company of Bellapart. We had hoped that Kevin Roche, being a Modernist architect, would seize the opportunity of the glass bars. But he judged the first technical proposal with the stainless steel tubes so favourably ("excellent work") that the experimenting with glass tubes was not carried any further. Also, the Spanish co-architect of Kevin Roche was afraid of the glass studs so the steel compression studs were used in the end as being too experimental for this project.

Fig. 165 Octatube proposal for 30 m circular glass roof for the main building at Santander Group City, Madrid, architect Kevin Roche, 2004.

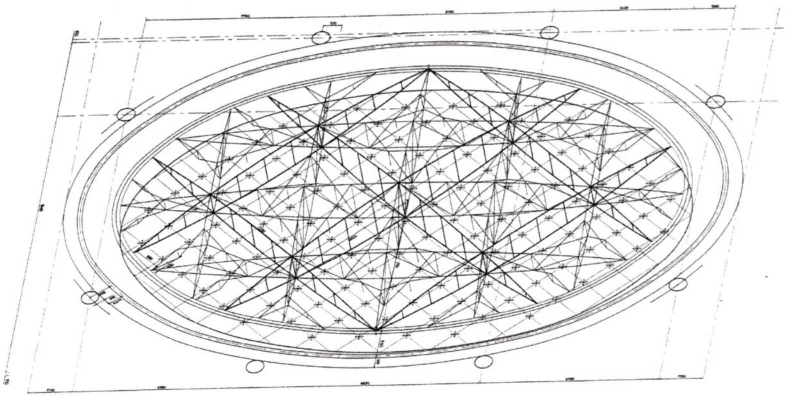

Fig. 166 An earlier Octatube attempt with glass studs for a shopping center in Magdeburg, Germany, not realized.

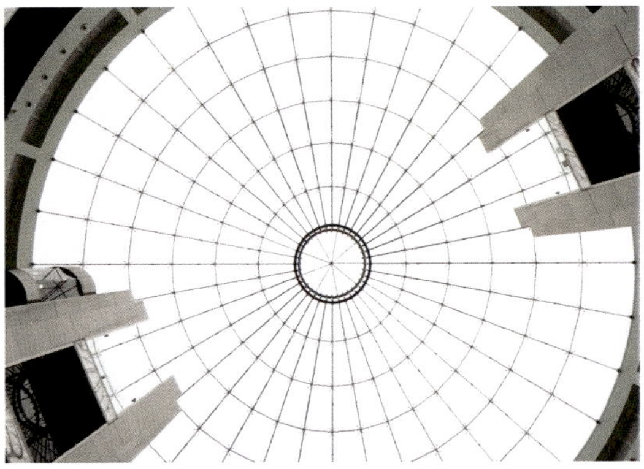

Left: Fig. 167 Interior view of Santander Group City main building.

Right: Fig. 168 Roof structure with steel compression studs.

Fig. 169 Perspective view from below.

CHAPTER 5.5

Square Spider Web Structures

Starting with diagonal arrangements of trusses, a stabilization system on a square ground plan, subdivided into 3 × 3 m, 4 × 4 m, 5 × 5 m or 6 × 6 m glass panels was developed. The tensile rod trusses always end in the corners of the square frame. Normally they are directly connected to a surrounding tubular framework, so that the tubes are (almost) only stressed in compression, while the rods are stressed in tension. These diagonal arrangements can be repeated to cover larger surfaces. The micro stabilization is then complimented by a macro arrangement of intersecting horizontal tubes supported at each crossing by columns or by flying studs. These square diagonal spider web arrangements of tensile trusses were used in several projects. The first one was the roof and façade construction for the Shopping Centre Overvecht, Utrecht, designed by ONB architects in 1996. It had a supporting column grid of 8 × 8 m.

In 1999 a free spanning atrium covering was also developed as a square tensegrity structure, sized 28 × 28 m and forming the atrium roof for a historical office building on Droogbak inAmsterdam dating back to the 19th century. The impressive building housed the Netherlands Architecture Institute and then accommodated offices for various law firms. The refurbishment was done by architect Joop van Stigt and the interior courtyard was covered as part of this refurbishment. The roof was subdivided into modules of 4 x 4 m panels, each sized 2 × 2 m, so module sizes of 8 × 8 m.

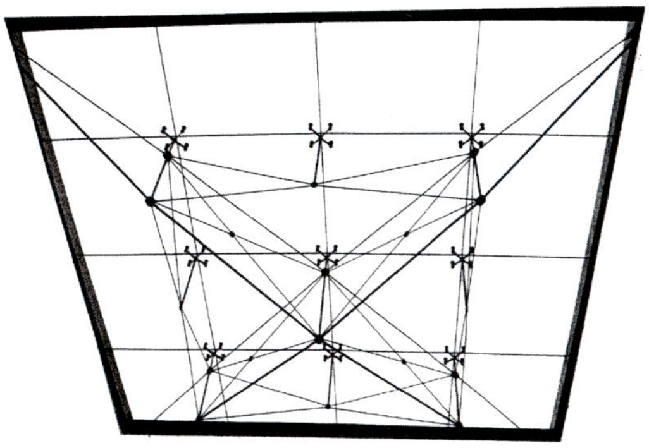

Fig. 170 Principle tensegrity scheme within square frame of tubular steel.

Fig. 171 Outside edge details of tensegrity glass at Shopping Centre Overvecht, Utrecht, architect ONB, 1996.

Fig. 172 Interior view of Shopping Centre Overvecht, Utrecht, OBN Architects 1996.

These modules were given a tubular structure stiffened by a system of lower tensile rods and vertical outriggers. Together they form a stiff and stable macro structure. The 8 × 8 m modules are subdivided by a tensile micro system.

The atrium cover is a diagonal spider web roof. The roof of 24 × 28 m was subdivided in squares of 4 × 4 m panels of each around 2.2m2, with a diagonal bracing of tensile rods. The macro tubular frame in itself had a similar tensile stabilization. The difference was that the horizontal forces from the macro frame had to be supplied by the attic floor of the building, which was built in wood. So the entire attic floor level had to be provided with diagonal strip bracings to supply the required horizontal forces. V-shaped gutters have been positioned above the tubular elements. Each macro square has its four-sided slope.

Fig. 173, 174 Overall view and details of the covered atrium at the historical office building on Droogbak, Amsterdam, architect Joop van Stigt, 1999.

The design competition for an atrium roof in the Frisian Nature Museum in Leeuwarden, The Netherlands, was won by architect Jelle de Jong, based in Lemmer, in collaboration with Octatube. The idea was to transform the outside courtyard of a 17th and 19th century building into a more protected public space. By covering the open courtyard, the town of Leeuwarden has been enriched with a glass covered town piazza. This space is often rented out for public occasions.
The roof structure is supported completely independent of the historical buildings surrounding it by means of four independently stabilized guyed masts, each 19 m high. The steel tubular masts are composed of a cylindrical middle part (406 mm diameter) with conical rolled parts above and below; the diameter of the upper part falls back to 50 mm. The roof is suspended at a height of 11 m with the aid of 4 × 8 mm cable rods, and below the glass 4 × 8 mm cable rods are used to pre-stress the roof supported by the columns. The horizontal macro-structure with a secondary 4 × 4 system of tensile trusses measures 25 m square.
The roof plane consists of 16 modules, each subdivided in 16 glass panels. Sixty automatic windows are distributed over the entire circumference of the roof for ventilation. They also provide a 'light touch' connection of the roof with the existing buildings. The insulated laminated glass panels were partially twisted on site in order to guarantee a slope of 3 degrees for draining rain water and for continuous detailing.

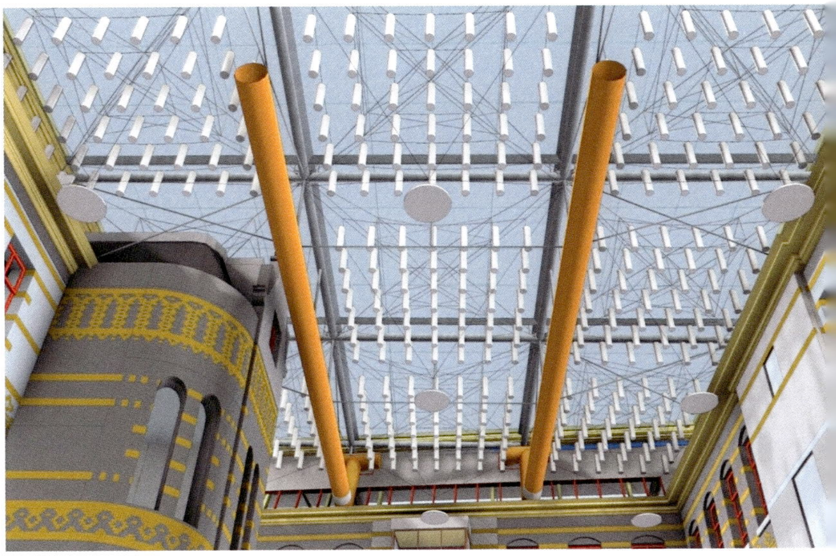

Top: Fig. 175 Octatube's proposal for sound absorbing baffles in line with the glass panel arrangement for renovation in 2021, architect KCAP.

Bottom: Fig. 176 Atrium interior of the Nature Museum Fryslân, Leeuwarden, architect Jelle de Jong, 2004.

CHAPTER 5.6
Glass Cubes

An example of a cubical glass building was realized in Tel Aviv as the entrance hall for the Tel Aviv Museum of Art, in collaboration with architect Dan Eytan. The structural system is tubular. The size of the cube is 12 m3. The structure of this glass cube relies on the principle of tensile trusses, interwoven in two directions and resulting in reaction forces in the four corners of the tubular structure, so that tubes again contain compression forces mainly and tensile truss elements only tension.

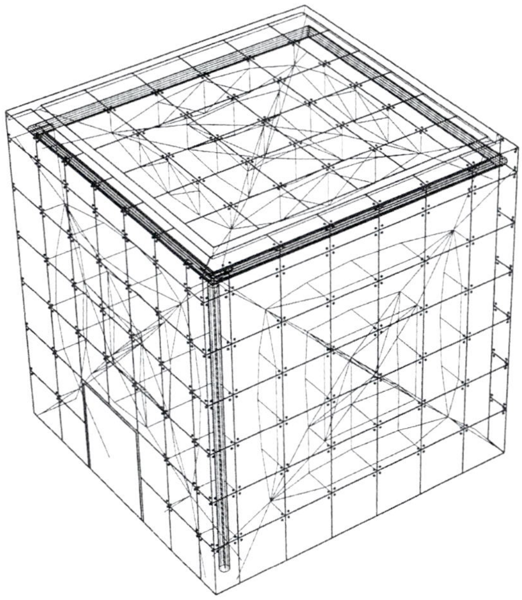

Fig. 177 Schematic drawing of the Tel Aviv Museum of Art entrance hall.

Fig. 178 Interior details of the entrance glass cube for the Tel Aviv Museum of Art.

Opposite page: Fig. 179 Interior view of the Tel Aviv Museum of Art entrance hall, architect Dan Eytan, 1999.

Fig. 180 Cross section of the glass cube for Santander Bank, Madrid, architect Alfonso Millanes, 2008.

Fig. 181 Interior of the Santander Bank glass cube, Madrid, architect Alfonso Millanes, 2008.

As the prominent entrance building for the headquarters of the Santander Bank in Madrid, architect Alfonso Millanes designed a 30 m3 glass cube. Much of Octatube's earlier experiences with this kind of structure informed the design: Glass panels regular 2.5 × 2.5 m as quite big insulated and in the roof laminated glass panels with solar coatings. Top panels 3.5 × 2.5m. The steel structure trusses form 'fish-bones' of steel tubes and tensile rods on both sides.

In 2004, the Santander Group City near Boadillo del Monte, northwest of Madrid, was designed by architect Kevin Roche, New Haven. The complex houses some 6,000 employees. Within this development, the main building was conceived by Roche while Octatube proposed, detailed and realized its 30 m diameter circular glass roof. The roof proved an eye opener for the client in respect to lightweight slender structures.

Some years later Santander wanted an all-glass cube to serve as the entrance for the bank's headquarters. Madrid architect Alfonso Millanes developed the cube, drawing on the expertise of the engineering offices of Typsa and Octatube. The predominant features of this building were a 30 × 30 m floor plan, a height of 21.4 m, the use of 2.5 x 2.5 m Insulated Glass Units (IGU), large custom-designed Quattro nodes 350 × 350 mm, a compression tube grid of 5 × 5 m, a loadbearing glass structure with integrated wind braces, a mechanical connection between glass and nodes through the inner plate of each IGU, twisted roof panels, an insulated glass roof gutter as well as an integrated water drainage system.

A completely flat roof can only exist in theory since rain water needs to be drained off to prevent stains on the glass, or even worse, excessive accumulation of water on the surface of the roof. The roof was designed to drain water to the gutter located on all four sides, thus raising the central area. The glass panels of the roof are cold twisted to avoid the use of triangular glass panels. The glass gutter is positioned directly above one of the compression tubes of the main steel structure. This not only disguises the gutter, but also leaves the corner of the roof-façade connection to be very transparent as well; only a mechanical glass-on-glass connection is used to support this corner. The vertical corners of the cube are designed in a similar fashion; the main difference being the use of a vertical corner profile to support the weight of the glass panels.

Fig. 182 Quattro node detail in the façades.

Fig. 183 Roof detail of the Santander Bank glass cube, Madrid.

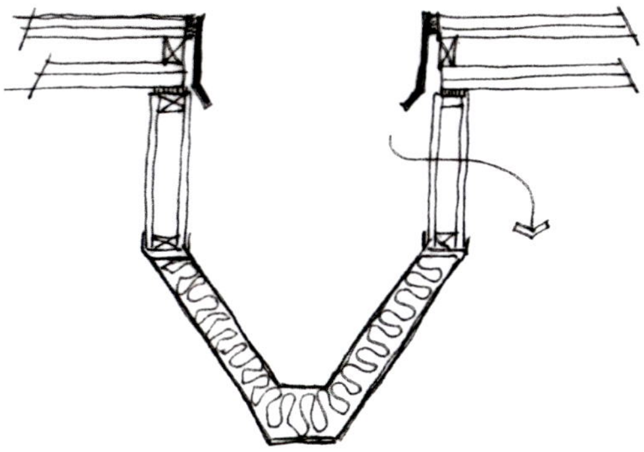

Fig. 184 Sketch of roof detail with gutter. The upper parts of the gutter are made in insulated glass components to visually minimize the gutters in counterlight.

Previous pages:
Fig. 185 Interior view of the Santander Bank glass cube, Madrid, architect Alfonso Millanes), 2008.

Fig. 186 Design of industrial designer Maxim Eekhout in his graduation project for a maintenance robot driven by steam and operable from the ground level by a joystick. This façade cleaning robot was subsequently developed further.

Fig. 187 Details of Santander Bank glass cube of Madrid.

The integration of several functions into the components comprising the structure of the cube was imperative to reach the accomplished transparency level. For instance, the wind bracings of the main structure not only served to stabilize the structure against horizontal external forces, but are also designed to support the glass panels on the façade. As customary at Octatube, the structure was prefabricated as much as possible in the Delft factory. This, together with the just-in-time arrival of components on the building site, leads to a short and effective assembly. This also applies to the glass panels; they are delivered to the site with little lead-time to minimize the risks of damage during storage at the building site. Thus all glass panels, 516 in total, were assembled without any damage. The Santander Bank glass cube testifies to Octatube's high degree of expertise gained over more than 30 years. From an engineering point of view, the glass cube structure realized in Madrid is the about as light a construction as possible.

As a next step, it might be interesting to explore the use of glass panels for the absorption of shear forces in the plane of the façade and the roof or to provide the glass panels with internal tubes so that vertical pre-stressed cables could be inserted through the panes to stabilize the façade against wind pressures.

Fig. 188 The exterior of the Santander Bank glass cube by night.

CHAPTER 5.7
Façades as Tensile Membranes

At times, architectural design is too ambitious for what is technically feasible. But at other times, ideas arise that bring the entire designing & building team to a higher level. For example, glass panels have become larger and larger over a number of years. The only limiting factor is the production process itself. Other limitations originate from deflections by wind and snow loads from ever growing spans despite the growing glass thickness. For many years, jumbo glass panels had a width of 2.14 m and a length of 3.60 m, determined by the size of the tempering oven and the lamination autoclave. Thus, one-storey high panels had a maximum height of 3.6 m. The initial solution would be to support the 3.6 m high panels on l/5th of their spans from both ends (720 mm), so that they have a cantilevering scheme. (An example of this approach is the Prinsenhof Museum glass hall on page 96) For a width of 1.8 m to 2.0 m the necessary glass panel thickness under 1.0 kN wind pressure would be 10 mm for façades. The deflection preferably within the thickness of the glass panel. If on the other hand the façade span would be a blunt 3.6 m in height (full office storey height), the deflection of a 10 mm thick panel would be as much as 200 mm! This could be reduced by fixing the panel connectors 720 mm from the corners. The deflection would then only be 50 mm, but thanks to considerable vertical stresses on the connection points.

An example of a large frameless glass façade without a stiff loadbearing sub-structure is represented

by the well-known Kempinski Hotel at Munich Airport, designed by architect Helmut Jahn and

engineered by Jörg Schlaich. Its façades are 30 m wide and 12 m high, made up of 1.8 × 1.8 m panels.

The loadbearing structure is a single pre-stressed cable net structure. This structural concept allows

for large horizontal deflections and relies on special dilatation connections to the side of the glass

façade and the stiff building parts. In some areas, due to large deformations, the fully tempered glass panels would be subjected to a twisting deformation. As to my knowledge the project was never granted a building permit but nevertheless, thanks to the personality of Jörg Schlaich, it was realized. And widely copied all over the world.

INHOLLAND UNIVERSITY OF APPLIED SCIENCES, DELFT

In 2009, we realized a similar scheme for three 13 m high façades of the INHolland University of Applied Sciences in Delft, designed by architect Rijk Rietveld, New York. Wind stabilization was achieved by means of vertical pre-stressed aramid cables. The idea was to split coping with deadweight from coping with wind loading. The calculated deflections of the 13 m high façades due to wind loads are 330 mm inward and outward. The acceptable level of pre-stress of the aramid cables influenced the upper steel structure which had to be reinforced. It is necessary to check the pre-stress level of the cable regularly. The composite laboratory at INHolland originally requested composite framing for the double glass panels and composite (carbon fibre reinforced epoxy) tubes for the feeding through of the aramid cables through the centres of the double glass panels. However, the adhesion tests of the different sealants did not prove easy. Delamination occurred quite often and in this case long-term and very reliable tests have to be conducted before an industrial product can be guaranteed. The glass manufacturer Asahi Glass Company did not have enough time to perform the necessary double glass composite adhesion tests and thus refused their usual guarantee. That was reason enough to change the design in the very last minute.

Fig. 189 The completed pre-stressed glass façades from the exterior, architect Rijk Rietveld, 2009.

All-glass façades for larger spans need stabilizing systems for wind and deadweight loads. Frameless façades show ultimate visual lightness as daylight is not hindered by obstructing steel purlins and aluminium framing profiles. In an experimental process of design and development of a composite façade for the INHolland University of Applied Sciences in Delft a system was selected and developed in which pre-stressed cables were to take up horizontal wind forces while deadweight suspension rods transferred the vertical deadweight of the system. Both pre-stressed cables and suspension rods were initially designed to be located within the thickness of the insulated glass panels. The prestressed aramide cables are located inside the tubes in the inner spaces of the double glass units, while the suspension rods are located in the end zones, that is the seams between the panels. The process highlights the many hindrances and risks involved in such a dense integration of the two independently developed 'alien' components: the double glass units and the pre-stressed cables. The experimental design scheme and the engineering response to it are described here.

Fig. 190 Overall view of the full-size façade segment mock-up showing the cables running through the glass cavity.

Fig. 191 Detail view of the mock-up: the aramid cable clamp with pre-stress mechanism.

Because of the cables penetrating the spacer of the insulated glass, special holding carbon tubes were installed, sealed off airtight, to create an airtight box of the insulated glass. The second function of the tubes, in a part of the façade, was to transfer the deadweight of the façade to the foundation as the tubes protruded from the insulated glass panels and the deadweight would be transferred by stacking the glass panels on top of each other. Thus, the tubes had two functions: holding the cable and transmitting deadweight. the dimensions of the tube, cable and spacer had to be synchronized with extremely small tolerances.

The composite spacers had to be developed to obtain a real overvalue of the composite spacers over the metal ones. The end of the first experimental design phase was the full-size façade mock-up in the factory of Octatube, on the other side of the street as the INHolland building under construction. The mock-up was used for gaining experience with prestressing of the aramide cables and stacking and tolerances of the glass panels. The glass panels have dilatations in every horizontal seam. Much attention was given to the corner detail, which was realized in a flexible rubber sandwich laminate. Bearing in mind that both of the large façades could be pushed inside simultaneously by wind pressure, the corners were given a lens-shaped rubber connection, an insulated rubber sail as it were. In all possible loading situations the rubber corners can deform and keep the glass panels undamaged. The deadweight is taken up by stainless steel deadweight suspenders (with saddles to catch the deadweight of each glass panel individually) in between the vertical seams, sealed off by silicone sealant on both sides.

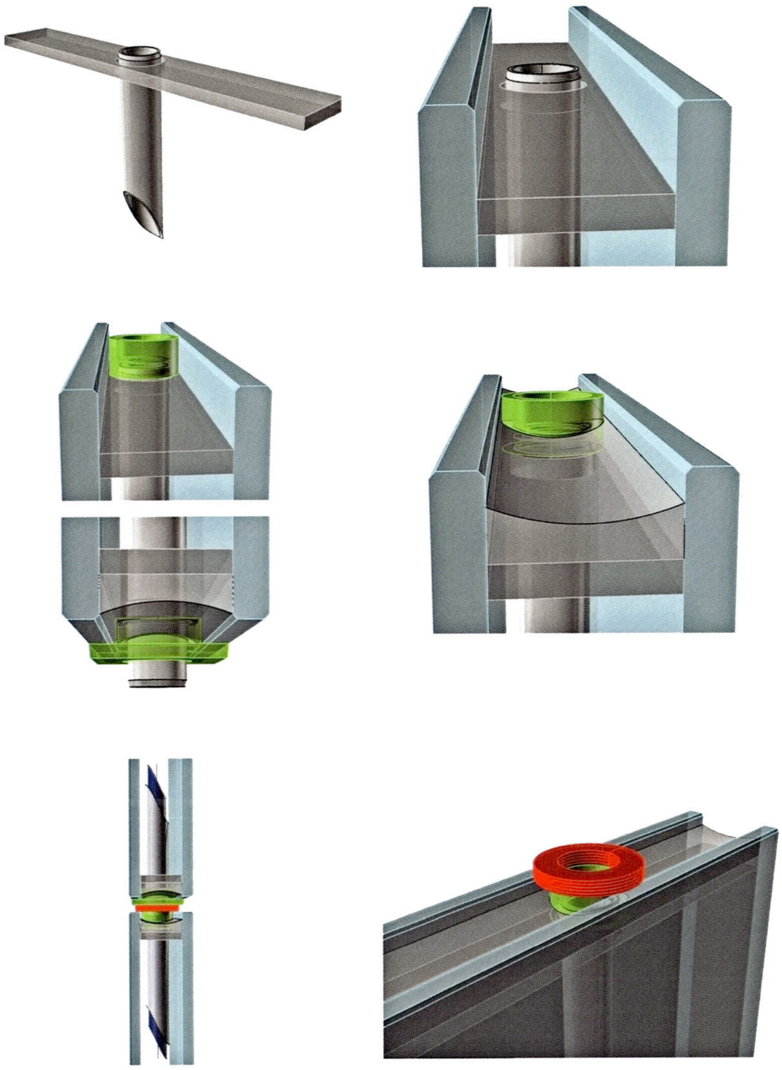

Fig. 192 Engineering concept showing the aramid cables inside the double glass panel.

At the very last moment, just before starting the production of the glass panels Asahi Glass Company decided not to give the usual no-delamination guarantee on the engineered glass panels. Therefore, in the two large façades the aramid cables had to be positioned on the interior face of the DGU panels instead of in the center of the inner space. The third façade, only 3 m wide, was realized as per the original design. It acts as the truly experimental façade in which all climatic and adhesion aspects are monitored regularly. The glass panel manufacturer had discovered that the short-term tests did not provide satisfactory results as to the airtightness of the tube-to-frame connections and the airtightness of the carbon fibre tubes themselves on the long term. This potentiality, however, could easily lead to the necessity of the complete replacement of the entire façade when the insulated glass panels would indeed show air leakages after some time. The replacement had to be done on costs of the supplier within 10 years and on costs of the client after that date. Bot supplier and client saw their own responsibility. In a dramatic week in May 2009, the author took the decision to reposition the cables from the inside of the double glass units to the outside, in the inners space of the building in fact, with the carbon fibre mantle tubes to the inside of the space, adjacent to the insulated glass panels. So with this engineering manoever factory guarantees were given again, but the project had again lost one of its innovative potentialities.

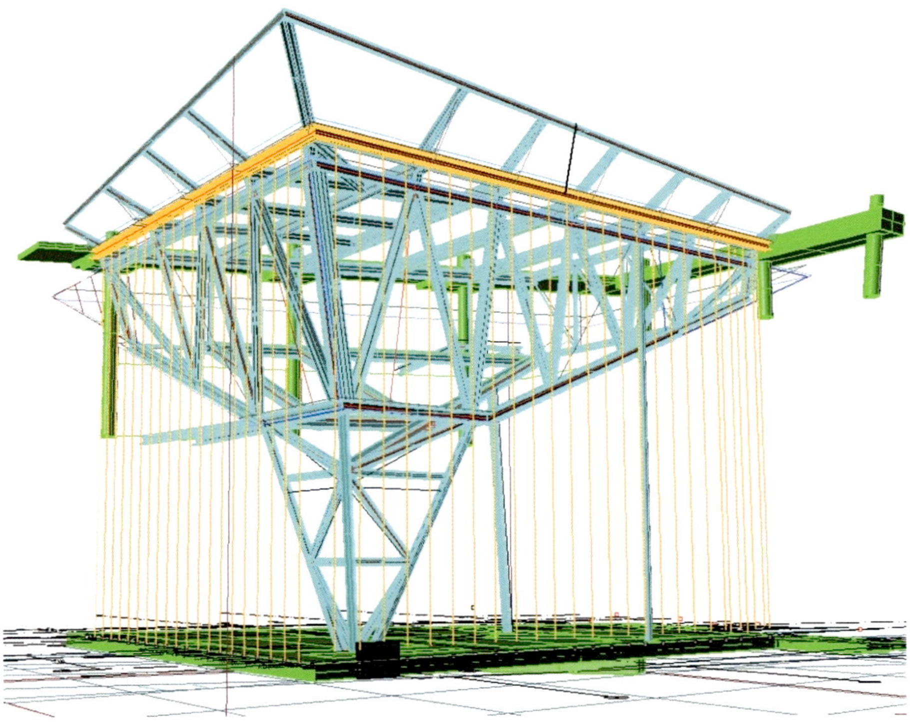

Fig. 193 3D view of overall steel structure with post-stressed aramide cables.

Left: Fig. 194 Interior view of the INHolland cable façade with the rubber corner. On the left hand side the original design façade.

Right: Fig. 195 Outside view of the INHolland cable façade again with the rubber corner.

Left: Fig. 196 Details of the composite façade part, where carbon fibre epoxy double glass frames and tubes were used to allow the aramid cable to stabilize the façade vertically against wind loadings.

Right: Fig. 197 Interior view of the InHolland glass façade. The façade realized according to the original concept with integrated aramide cables is visible on the left side.

CHAPTER 5.8

Cable-Stayed Glass Façades for Market Hall

The 'Markthal' or Market Hall in Rotterdam as designed by architect Winy Maas of MVRDV and developed by Hans Schröder of Provast [ref.31] as the project developer, consists of an envelope in cylindrical form wrapped around an atrium, in which a daily vegetable market is located. The building accommodates 228 apartments. Needless to say, only the lower 3 m of the 35 m height of the inside hall can be used by people. As a sign of the vegetable market the inner walls and ceiling are decorated by giant colourful fruits and vegetables, so that the function of the cathedral-like space cannot be easily ignored. The two façades on the front and rear end of the cylinder are the largest windows in The Netherlands. From the inside looking out they give a spectacular view over Rotterdam, towards the 'Blaak' side and the town side.

In the townscape of Rotterdam the market hall is located near the Great or Saint Lawrence Church, a Gothic church that was completely restored after the German bombing of Rotterdam's city center at the beginning of the Second World War. It could be argued that in both buildings the required workmanship in their days were high-tech: The Protestant church, once built as a Catholic basilica, was the first stone building in Rotterdam. The central vault could be fitted completely into the market hall space. The Market Hall stands out within the townscape of Rotterdam due to its unusual shape.

Fig. 198 Markthal, Rotterdam, architect MVRDV, 2014, rendering

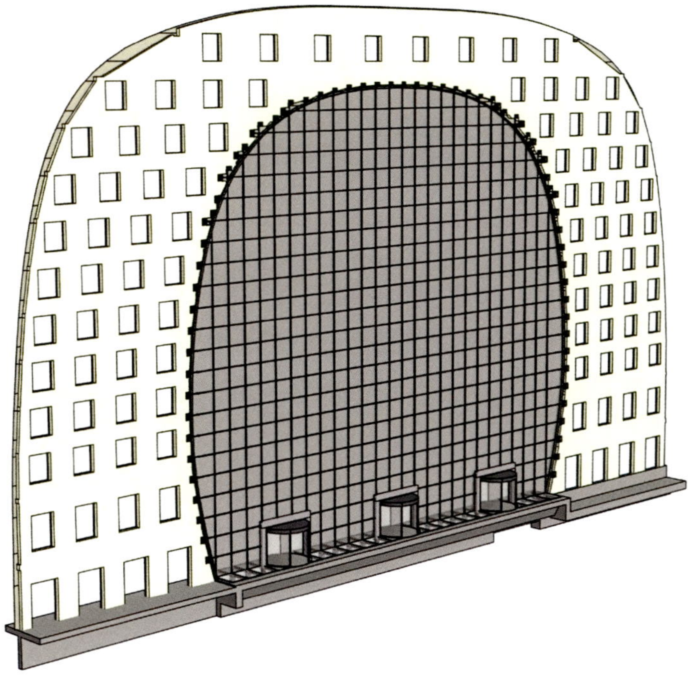

Fig. 199 Engineering model of cable net façade.

TECHNICAL BASIS

The cylindrical apartment building was closed off on both sides by a vertical glass façade, the largest in The Netherlands: 42 m wide and 35 m high. The loadbearing structure is a single-layer steel cable net structure, highly pre-stressed and provided with laminated glass panels to create an extremely slender and transparent glass façade.

The module of the cable net dictates the size of the glass panels. In this project the cable net with all of its design considerations and engineering analysis is far more intriguing than the glass panels.

But there are actually three matters of interest for a scientific audience in the glass world:

- The behaviour of the glass panels in high wind, especially in the four corners, where large distortions in the individual glass panels may occur;
- The relation between the pre-stressed or 'over-stressed' cable net and de-stressing creep in the concrete frame surrounding together with deformations in the subsoil;
- Pre-stressing and de-stressing of the cable net and consequently the tolerances of the glass panels and its nodal points.

CABLE NET STRUCTURE CONSIDERATIONS

The two glass façades at either ends of the cylindrical space are surrounded by a 300 mm thick reinforced concrete façade structure in the same plane acting as an arch. In the basement, the arch is complemented by a concrete wall with some openings to a semi-circular border of concrete. There are uncertainties in the Rotterdam subsoil, which has been formed by the river Maas and its banks; the city's origins were a trading port that chose this former marsh delta with its watery environment for a permanent settlement. Piling into the sand layers below has to be as deep as 30 m. Actually, the soil is not particularly suited for high-rise buildings One of the problems was the soil 'layer of Kedichem' with its unknown properties, which were analyzed by DHV Engineers. Uneven soil deformations were accounted for and have influenced the design of the concrete frame surrounding the cable net glass façade.

Fig. 200 View of the cable net façade from inside to outside.

CREEP IN CONCRETE

One of the basic problems is creep of freshly poured concrete. It is a well-known engineering fact that reinforced concrete creeps for two years after its pouring. What would happen when the cable net was pre-stressed in the concrete frame, thus enlarging the creep phenomenon, while after two years the fully installed cable net structure with the glass panels would be released a bit due to the concrete creep?

However, the pre-stressing targeted was high enough to allow for a 2 % relaxation due to creep. The glass panels are not deformable, of course. The deformation has to come from the sealant zones, which in this case are not the usual 10–12 mm, but slightly larger: 12–16 mm. The choice of sealant allows permanent deformation due to creep.

TEMPERATURE LOADS IN THE CABLES

Another factor influencing the cables is temperature load: in summer the maximum temperature could be as high as 40 °C, and in winter may be 5 °C or even less. These temperature differences result in a temperature load. The pre-stress value of 250–300 kN per cable has an over-stress value of 50 kN to cope with the above-mentioned three de-stressing causes (soil deformation, creep in concrete and temperature load). The cables of the cable net are spaced 1,485 mm vertically and horizontally.

The cables are pre-stressed between strong (60 mm thick) steel boxes cast in the concrete walls with tolerances applicable in the concrete contracting, but with a tighter expectation. The boxes have been designed in such a way that the tolerances needed to construct a glass façade, which are much tighter than can be expected from poured concrete, can be met. The cables run through spherical joints to allow for deformations and prevent material fatigue.Positioning the cables inside the boxes enabled the erecting crew to position them exactly at 1,485 mm centre to centre. All cables have a diameter of 31.3 mm, and their breaking strength is 884 kN. A cast steel node is placed where the cables cross each other, allowing the two cables to intersect and at the same time fastening the corners of the glass panels.

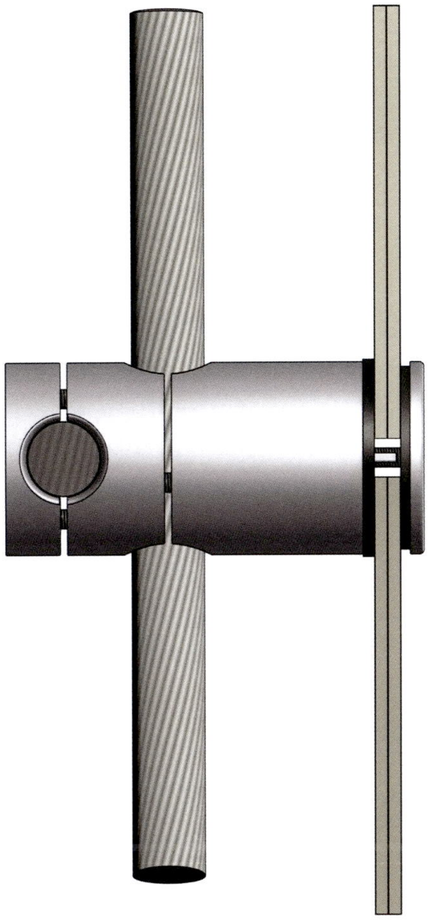

Fig. 201 Principal connection of cables and glass.

Fig. 202 Detail of the cable node.

Fig. 203 Mock-up of the left lower corner of the cable net façade.

Next page: Fig. 204 Interior photograph of the southern façade.

The cable net structure has also been analyzed for mishaps, like a truck driving into the lower part of the cable net, fire and a cable breakage. In addition to that, a wind force of up to 12 Beaufort, asymmetrical or in a rotating chess-like pattern, was taken into account.

ENTRANCES

The introduction of three portal frames around the rotating doors complicated the bottom of the cable net façade. These are the entrance doors to the market hall, also functioning as emergency exits in case of fire inside the market hall. The technology used is that of portal frames which can rotate inside and out, following the movement of the cables at all times. The upper rafter of the portal frame moves with the deformations of the cable net, while the two columns stay in the same position. The revolving doors, of course, stay vertical to allow entrance or exit by visitors and marketers. The portal frames and the turning doors are connected by a flexible collar to allow for the deformation of the cable net while letting the doors function properly. A design with a continuous horizontal member, placed on top of the revolving doors, would have made the 43 m long façade a lot easier to accomplish, but in order to fulfil the architectural ambitions, the façade continues to the ground level.

Top: Fig. 205 Cables rolled up before dispatch to the site.

Middle: Fig. 206 Post-stressing of the cables happened once they were exactly positioned.

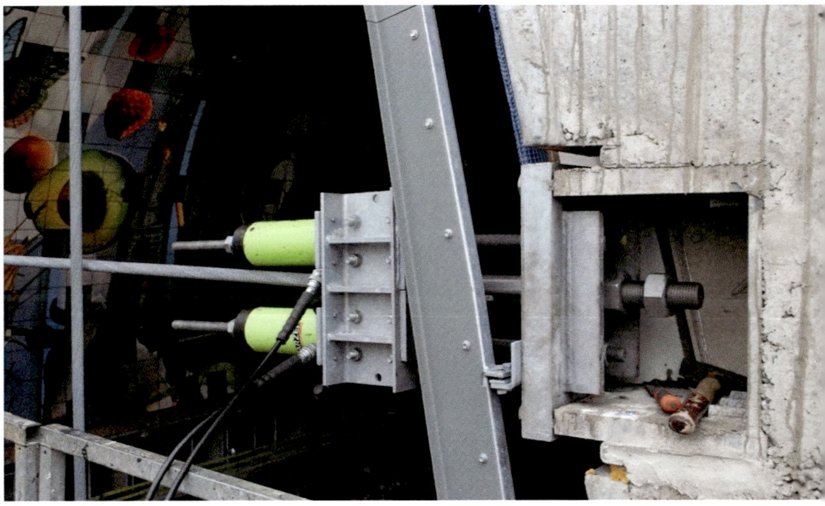

Fig. 207 The three entrances with the portal frames and the cable net glass façade.

When subjected to the highest wind load, a total elongation of 37 mm was calculated for the central cables, which results in a horizontal deformation in the centre of the cable net of 700 mm inward or outward (Fig. 208). In the centre of the cable net the rotation between two cable net parts or two glass panels is around 0.4 degrees. The rotation on the edges of the cable net is 1.9 to 5.4 degrees. These rotations are quite large, but for the regular sides, left and right and the top part, acceptable.

More complicated are the four corners. In principle in a corner, two sides are more or less fixed and the one corner of the glass panel directed towards the deforming cable net moves inside or outside.
The largest deformations on an individual glass panel sized 1,485 × 1,485 mm is 50 mm. Cleaning of the glass façade has to be done by an outside telescopic crane and on the inside by an overhead crane rail.

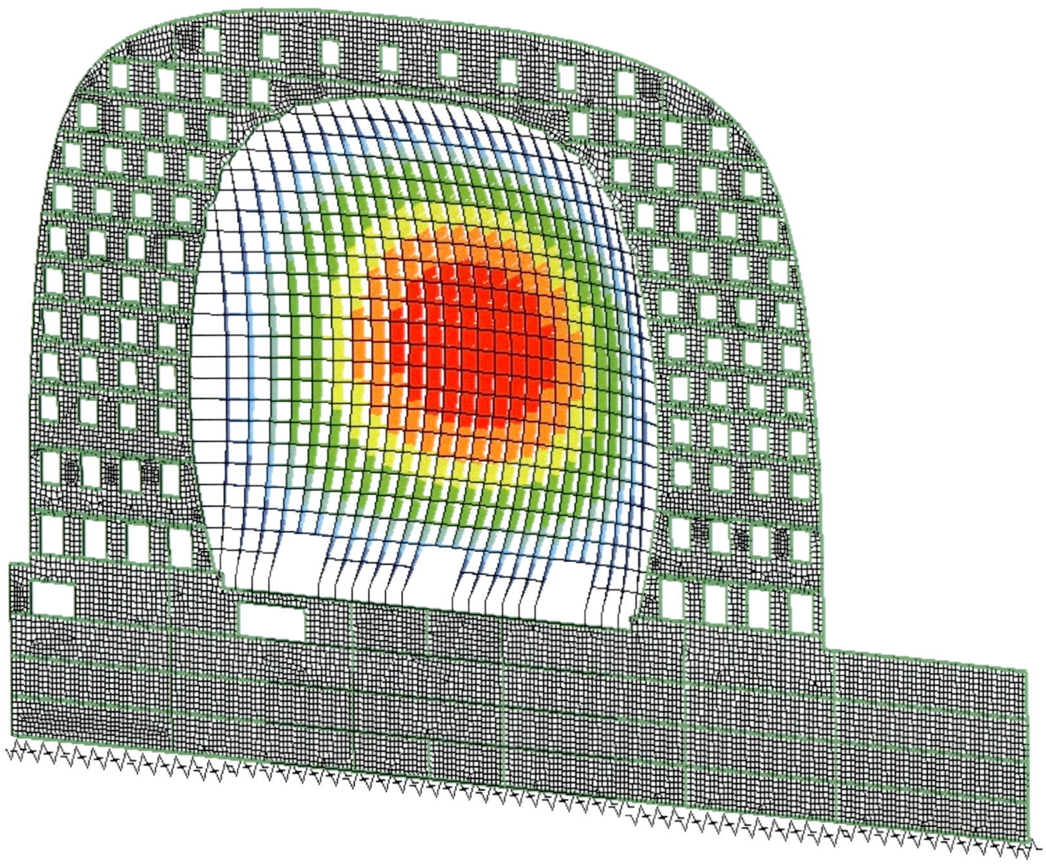

Fig. 208 Deformations during extreme wind loads maximum 700 mm inward during wind pressure and 700 mm outward during wind suction.

The erection of the cable net glass façade was completed in the spring of 2014. The cables were pre-stretched. The steel boxes were cast in concrete and the contractor assessed the misplacement tolerances. They were within the tolerances foreseen by the detailing of the boxes due to the later drilling of the face plates. The concrete roof of the cylinder was the last part to be poured into position, after a curing time of three months. Only after that the anchoring of the vertical cables and later the horizontal cables could be undertaken. It was assumed that the extra silicone sealant width of 16 mm compared to the regular 10–12 mm would give enough room when creep occured above expectations.

Fig. 209 Cable-stayed glass façade of Market Hall by night.

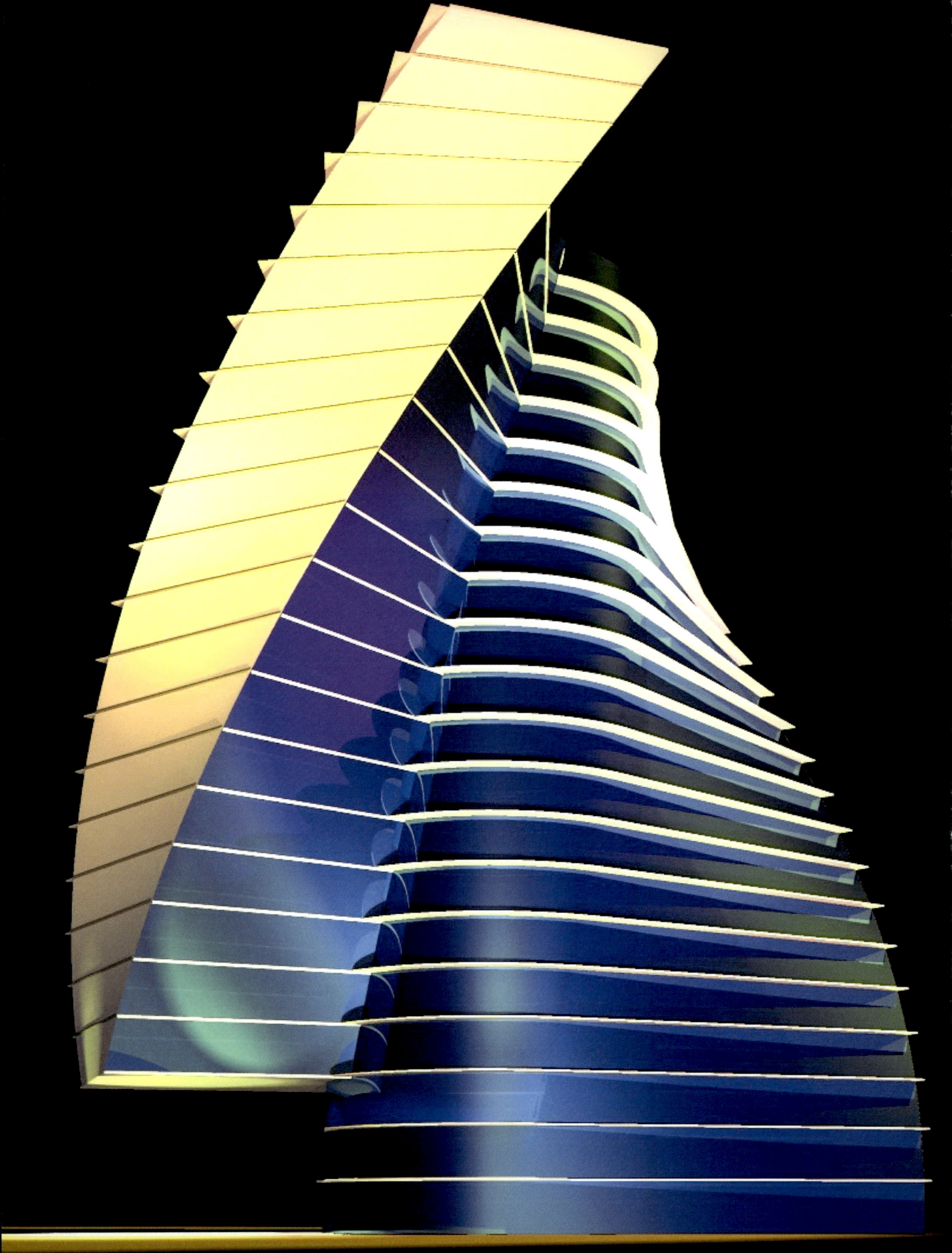

CHAPTER 6.
DEVELOPMENTS IN FREE-FORM TECHNOLOGY

Around 2000, the free-form or Blob technology became a research focus in Delft. Both at the TU Delft as well as at Octatube, a number of projects were investigated that extended the state of the art of glass in architecture. PhD student Karel Vollers received his doctorate in 2001 for his dissertation 'Twist & Build' on the urban and architectural design of twisted buildings [Ref. 24]. He developed the necessary building technical tools for twisted buildings. He researched and developed the material specifications of casting in deformed moulds or deforming flat plates, the production engineering of hot deformed or twisted glass and the window details. He also designed twisted buildings. Several architects have designed twisted buildings after the publication of Dr. Vollers in 2001, and certainly Santiago Calatrava's design for the Turning Torso in Malmö, 2005, could have been inspired by Vollers's work. He could even be called the godfather of twisted building around the world.

Karel Vollers continued his research work by exploring the hot deformation of glass panels with an industrially usable mould. The mould consists of mechanically adjustable pins with a flat, rotating surface and a device to smoothen the surface the tops describe. Together with a heat-resistant glass fibre mat a temporary surface is created on which the hot glass pane can be placed before cooling off.

Opposite page: Fig 210 Design proposal by Dr. Karel Vollers for highrise in Dubai in his dissertation 'Twist & Build', 2001.

Fig. 211 Proposal for twisted office towers in Amsterdam by Karel Vollers.

Fig. 212 Mock-up of a twisted façade as developed by Karel Vollers for Reynolds.

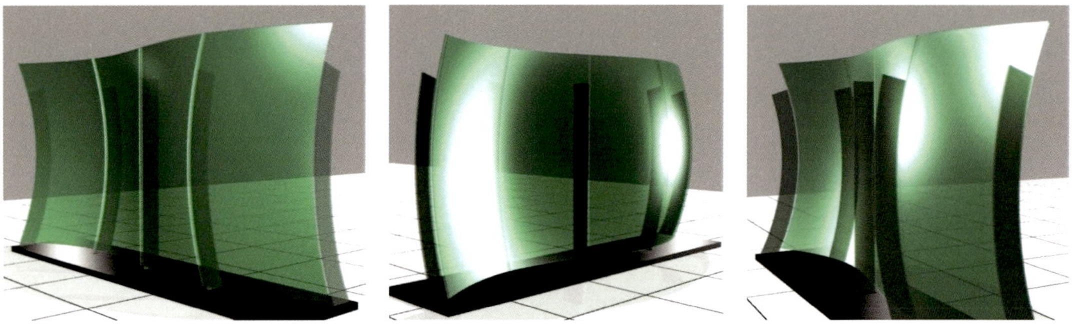

Fig. 213 Designs of thermally deformed glass panels from a reusable jig as developed by Karel Vollers and PhD student Daan Rietbergen.

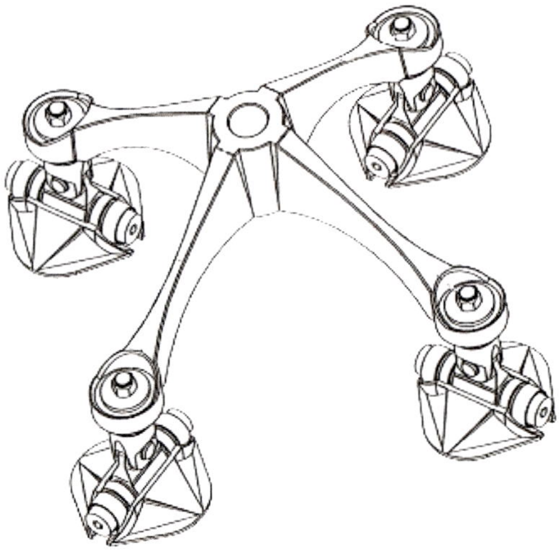

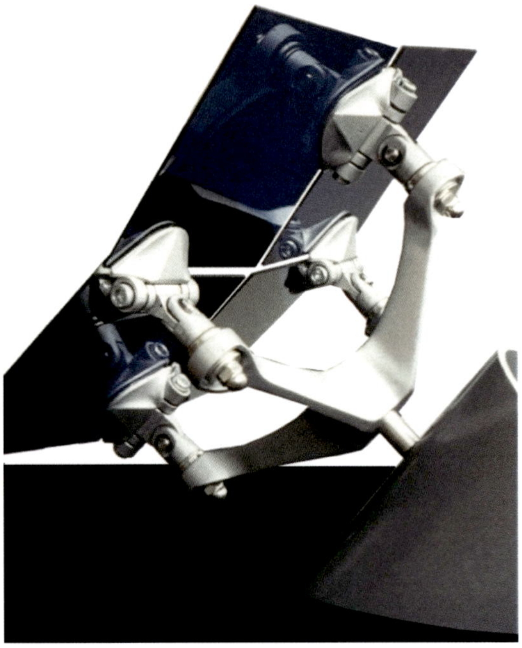

Fig. 214, 215 Quattro node with glued connection developed by graduation student Barbara van Gelder.

Graduation student Barbara van Gelder did her final thesis at Octatube and developed a glued connection for a multi-facetted façade. This design was flexible in its corners so that polygonal bodies of buildings could be accommodated. She also did a project with glued nodes in frameless glazing in this same period in Brussels and currently works as a design engineer at Octatube. The highly flexible, fluid nodes she had designed were to be used in the Malmö greenhouse described in chapter 6.13, p.156. However, during the development of the project, a less prominent nodal design was looked for and finally a node bolted through the seams between the glass panels was chosen.

CHAPTER 6.1
Cold Twisted Glass Panels

The back part of the Town Hall of Alphen aan den Rijn, The Netherlands, designed by architect Erick van Egeraat, had a double curved surface with glass lintels. As these glass lintels did not run concentrically, many of the composing glass panels had to be twisted. The initial solution was to work with timber frames and flat glass panels and saw-tooth triangles in between, a similar concept as used for the façades of the Neue Staatsgalerie in Stuttgart, 1983, by James Stirling. However, the timber window frame producer found it impossible to develop such a solution for Alphen and Octatube was asked for an alternative.

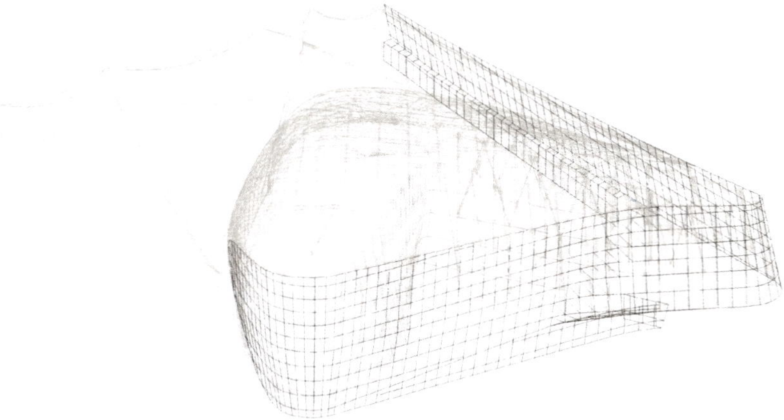

Fig. 216 Twisted front façade and overall digital view of the Town Hall, Alphen aan den Rijn, 2003, architect Erick van Egeraat..

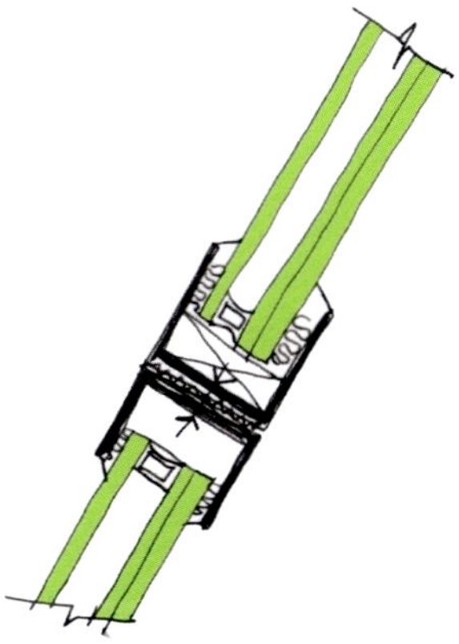

Fig. 217 Detail scheme of the cold twisted glass panels. Panels are shifted upwards, twisted by hand and lowered in the twisted sill profile.

Fig. 218 Spaghetti façade with cold twisted glass at the back of the Town Hall in Alphen.

Opposite page:
Fig. 220 Exterior view of Town Hall Alphen.

The idea here was to make a frameless glass system and to twist all glass panels on site. However, the frames caused problems. Their upper and lower profiles were stiff U-channels. The insulated glass panels were at maximum 900 × 2000 mm large and consisted of an 8 mm outer blade fully tempered and an inner blade of also fully tempered 4.4.2 glass. The silicone seals were normal butt seals. The glass was twisted out of its plane maximally 40 mm. This concept proved to be realizable at very reasonable costs, although with larger risks than normal (potential breaking of panels on site was up 300 % compared to the normal practice).

After having completed the job, it was not clear how exactly it had been achieved. It took TU Eindhoven graduation student Dries Staaks one full year of work at the Octatube laboratory in Delft to discover and describe the regularities of cold twisting of glass panels, see chapter 6.2.

Fig. 219 Close-up view of the cold twisted glass panels in the front façade of the Town Hall in Alphen.

CHAPTER 6.2
Regularities of Cold Twisting of Glass

The theory behind the cold twisted double and laminated glass panels in the Town Hall of Alphen aan den Rijn, completed in 2003 (see chapter 6.1.), was taken up as a challenge by graduation student Dries Staaks. His task was to research and understand the regularities of cold twisting of glass. In the laboratory of Octatube he discovered that glass panels can be cold twisted elastically, deforming in a symmetrical way into a hypar surface as long as the enforced deformation out-of-plane is less than 16 times the panels' thickness. More twisting will evoke a change of deformation pattern resulting in unidirectional bending along the shortest (stiffest) diagonal axis.

Fig. 221, 222 Schemes of cold deformation between elastic behaviour and buckling and mock-up for testing.

This change in deformation is caused by an instability phenomenon. The double curvature of a twisted plate causes membrane forces: pressure in the middle and tension along the edges. With an increase of twisting, the membrane forces increase exponentially until the pressure causes the plate to buckle, resulting in the change of deformation. The amount of twisting at which instability occurs proved to be linear related to the panels' thickness, independent of material and size except for the length/width ratio. With small degrees of twisting stresses are uniformly distributed. This stress is linear related to the plates' thickness. A thinner plate will experience equally lower stress. With increased twisting, the stress will increase more than linear due to the growing influence of the membrane forces. In general, twisted geometries with a deformation of up to 10 % of the panels' width are possible when using pre-stressed glass. This theory can also be applied to massive plates like aluminium and steel sheets.

The increasing demand for free-form transparent building envelopes caused by the trend of fluid design in architecture was the main reason to start research on cold twisting of glass. A fluently shaped transparent building skin is commonly approached with a subdivision of triangular panels. The use of quadrangular panels is to be 38preferred for aesthetic and often also economic reasons. Typical for such a design in a free-form geometry is that one of the four corners of each quadrangle is out of plane, causing a twisted deformation of the panel. To a certain extent glass panels are capable of coping with this deformation in addition to deadweight, wind and snow load. For frameless glazing staying within the first deformation pattern is important because all edges remain straight and adjacent panels connect smoothly. Consequently the possibility of predicting the point of instability with its sudden change in deformation pattern became the main focus point of Staaks's research.

Based on a combination of empirical and numerical analysis, he developed his 'Theory of Staaks'. This theory predicts instability for materials, thicknesses, sizes and length/width ratios, summarised in the publication 'Cold Twisted Glass' by Dries Staaks 2012 [ref.25].

The gained knowledge about the structural behavior and the determined regularities in deformationand stresses do provide the architect, (structural) engineer with the necessary tools to apply this economically and production technically accessible technique in their latest design.

Fig. 223 Mock-up in the Octatube factory of a cold twisted, laminated, fully tempered glass panel 1.8 × 1.8 m, deformed 100 mm out of its original flat plane.

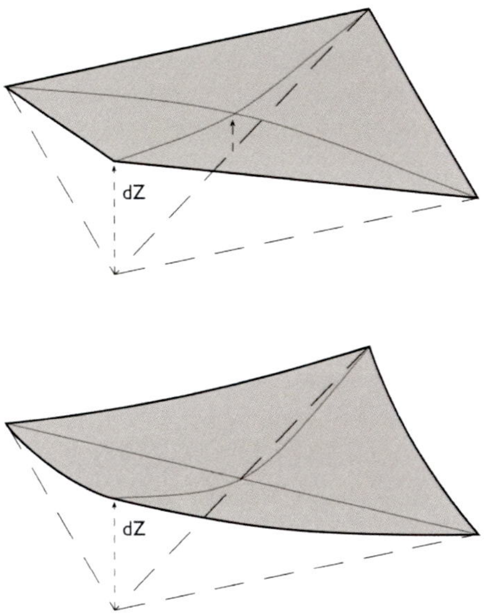

Fig. 224 In the first deformed shape the four edges of the plane remain straight; after the change of shape all edges are curved.

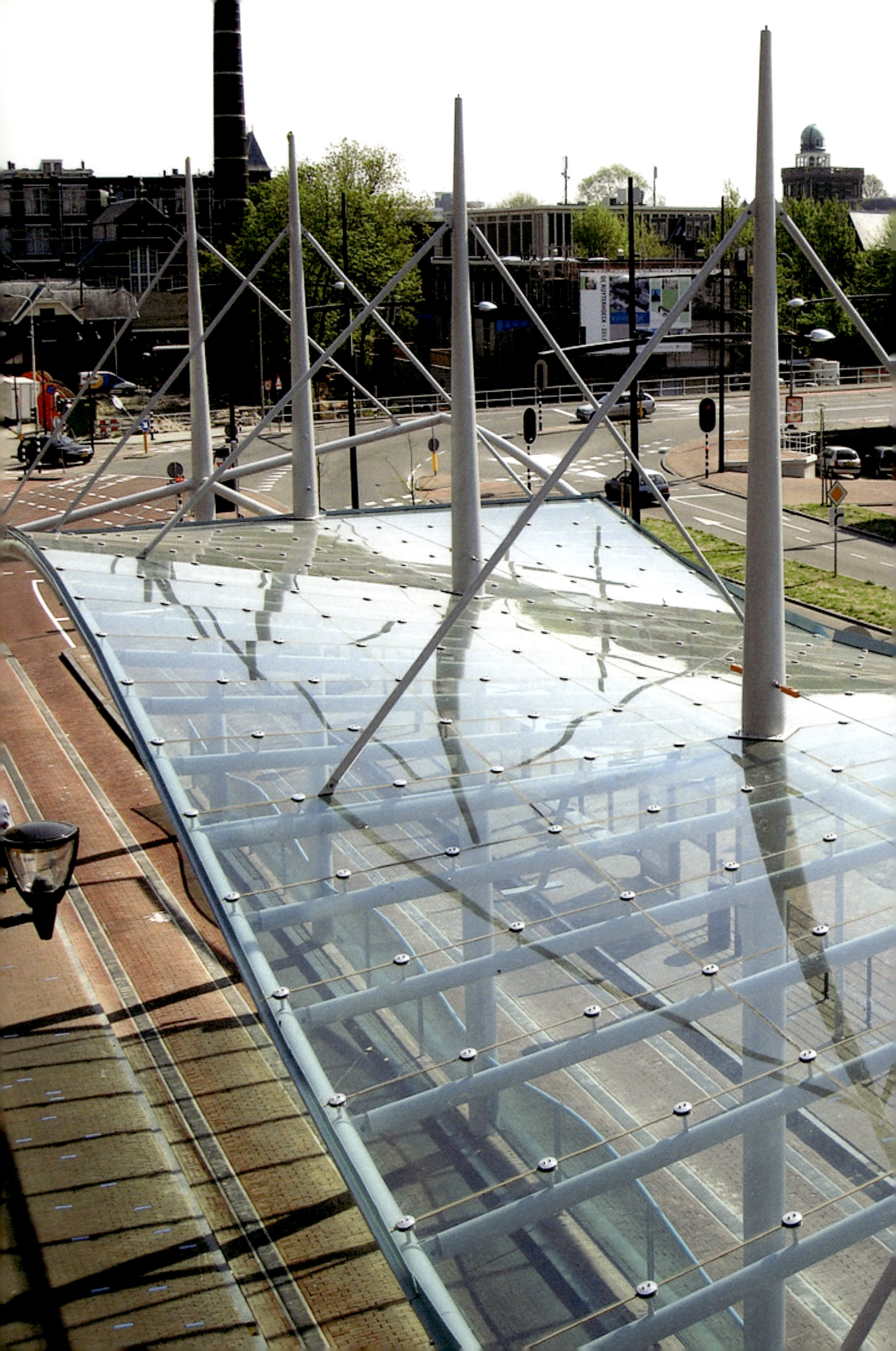

CHAPTER 6.3

Cold Twisted Glass in Tram Canopy 'Zuidpoort', Delft

At the south side of the centre of Delft, a new bus and tram station connecting the inner city with the TU Delft campus was built, part of a masterplan by the Belgian architect Bob van Reeth. The environment of shops and city apartments is quite dense in this area. Therefore we opted for a visually light undulating glass roof canopy suspended from masts with a free height of around 6 m to allow for the tram, and a width of 12 m; the length is 80 m, of which in total 60 m were glass covered. The design evokes the Delft coat of arms with its undulating lines, representing the connection with water and sea. Delft's harbour, Delfthaven, was the earlier harbour of Rotterdam. The undulating line fitted in with Delft symbolism and gave the opportunity to investigate the possibilities of cold twisted glass panels in a warped roof form. The roof consists of laminated glass, one pane 6 mm green float and one pane 6 mm clear float glass. Both panes were fully tempered and produced as standard flat panels. The main structure is tubular steel, hot dip galvanized and powder coated, and has stainless steel saddles on which the flat panels are laid and forced into the desired undulating form. On top, additional stainless steel saddles keep the panels in position by their pre-tension. The findings of Dries Staaks (see chapter 6.2) were fully exploited here. The result was a glass canopy produced with standard glass panels that creates an interesting and surprising undulating form.

Fig. 226 Undulating glass roof for bus and tram stop Zuidpoort in Delft, architect Mick Eekhout, 2006.

Opposite page: Fig. 225 Zuidpoort canopy with cold twisted glass.

Fig. 227 View of the glazed bus station canopy Zuidpoort.

In 2003, the triangulated façade of the Town Hall of Alphen (see chapter 6.1) could not be twisted hot, because of the screening and solar reflective coating on the inside of the double glass panels. Three years later, the twisting as cold deformed glass panels was possible, including the solar reflective coating and the screening. An area of 10 × 10 m could be twisted cold 2 m out of its plane. The combination of practical experience with theoretical research proved very fruitful.

A little devil on the shoulder whispers that this knowledge could be used in changing the polycarbonate panels of the cable net of the Olympic Roof of Munich by laminated glass, twisted cold in position and to flexibly deform with the cable net movements! As a contribution to a life long inspiration by prof.dr. Frei Otto.

Fig 228 Olympic Games roof (Frei Otto and Günther Behnish) with cable net roof covered by prestressed acrylic panels in 1972 could nowadays be covered with laminated fully tempered glass panels with more slender silicone sealant joints. Result of 50 years of incremental progress

CHAPTER 6.4

Twisted Glass Panels on Long Glass Fins

The super-slender tensile systems of Octatube (see chapter 5) were developed initially as an alternative for glass fins that originate from the 1960s. The technology of the tensile steel trusses gives glass architecture a high class of refinement. But some architects like to use glass fins because of their special appeal. One example is the Apple Cube in New York (architect Bohlin et al, 2006). Although its size is modest (12 × 12 × 12 m) the very location on Fifth Avenue makes it a prominent glass design. Glass fins should be tempered and laminated. The length/width ratio of glass fins makes them vulnerable to warping, which is undesirable, given the prominent visual function and the multilayering. Yet there are enough producers in Europe who produce good quality fins. The larger sizes (larger than 5 m) have to be produced in China.

In 2009, Muma Architects and Tim Macfarlane designed the Medieval & Renaissance Galleries of the Victoria & Albert Museum in London. The V & A, originally built in 1852, needed additional gallery space and decided to close off a horseshoe-shaped outdoor area, surrounded by Victorian buildings, by a glass roof. The upper rim of this roof was rectangular, while its lower rim was circular which meant that the glass surface of the sloped roof in between had to be twisted. However, the transparent roof should form a continuous glass plane.

Fig. 229 Top view of the curved glass roof with cold bent insulated glass panels in the day-lit Medieval & Renaissance Galleries of the V&A Museum, London, architect Muma Architects and engineer Tim Macfarlane, 2009.

Fig. 230 Piercing of glass fins through the Victorian decorative stonework with disguised support details in stainless steel and rubber behind.

Cold-twisting laminated insulated glass panels with three or four layers of fully tempered or heat-strengthened glass would need large manual forces. Also, high bolt forces were necessary to hold the twisted glass panels on their substructure which is normally metal. But one has to consider that glass fins are extremely vulnerable to high local forces. Screw and bolt forces coming from outside clamps on the glass surface are such high local forces. The solution was to introduce a stainless steel RHS profile, continuously sealed and bonded on the glass fin, able to accept the local forces from screwing or bolting and distribute these on the glass fin along the length of the metal profile. In an all-transparent glass roof a metal RHS profile is visible of course but no more than the black silicone sealant at the bottom and at the top of the metal. The metal profile remains in the shadow of silicone sealants.

These large fins were up to 11 m in length and they were inserted in the Victorian brickwork almost naively, without any details: very abstract. The fins appear to be cutting through the Victorian brickwork (or the sandstone parapet) as a knife would through butter (see fig. 230, page 162 and fig. 300, page 188). These fins needed of course complicated support shoes at their high ends, with soft bottom supports of EPDM rubber, but all this detailing is disguised behind the brickwork and stonework. For the glass fin PVB lamination, normally translucent, an opaque colour was chosen. That made the fins almost invisible at the height of 12 m. The form of the gallery space is high and narrow. Therefore, the fins are mostly viewed vertically upward and then appear transparent. But when seen tangentially, more in perspective, the fins are overlapping like coulisses for the theatre. When the colour would be whitish and translucent it would still be a roof. The effect was astonishing. Our practical experiences with cold twisted glass and the research of Dries Staaks (see chapter 6.2) allowed us to take on this special challenge. In 2010, the project received the Structural Design of the Year Award at the World Architecture Festival in Barcelona.

Next pages: Fig. 231 Interior view of the Medieval & Renaissance Gallery with cold twisted glass panels.

Fig. 232 Pavilion at horticultural show Floriade, Haarlemmermeer, architect Asymptote, 2002: water pond in frameless glazing bearing 1.4 m of water.

CHAPTER 6.5

An Application of Liquid Design in Glass

Over the last two decades a number of liquid design buildings have been realized with very complex 3D geometries and in some of them I was able to experiment with glass applications.

HEAVILY LOADED GLASS WATER POND

The glass water pond in one of the two roofs of the municipal Floriade pavilion in 2002, designed by Asymptote, New York, was loaded with 1.4 m high water, adding 14 kN weight/m² to the deadweight, the heaviest loading experienced by Octatube to date. It was originally designed as a 3D curved frameless glass composition. The glass would have been heated, curved in pairs, chemically pre-stressed and laminated with epoxy or acrylic resin. However, due to time limits it was realized only with flat laminated glass panels. The technical composition received an Honorable Mention at the DuPont Benedictus Awards 2003.

Fig. 233 Exterior view of Floriade Pavilion.

POINT-SUPPORTED COLD BENT GLASS

The south elevation of the Floriade pavilion has three large window glazings, each 6 × 6 m and composed of nine glass panels of roughly 2 × 2 m. The south windows are flat. The two side windows have a large curvature which was attained by cold bending of the flat laminated and fully tempered glass panels from their four corner connectors by screwing on two rubber pushers on the upper and lower edge, fixed on the curved steel CHS beam on the inside. Lamination was thought to be a safety precaution against sudden explosion in the face of the workers on the outside when stressing up the panels. However, no panel broke. The analysis resulted in high bending stresses: up to 50 % of the allowable bending stresses. The other 50 % were good enough for stresses from wind loads. Thus a system with an economical price and a curvature was realized. The radius to be attained in this way has to be larger than 4.5 m. Cold bending is worthwhile to be developed further as is employs cheap glass panel material and results in flowing shapes, provided it is done with a high level of engineering insight and experience (see also pages 12 and 13).

Figs. 234, 235 Interior and exterior view of the cold bent glass panels of the Floriade Pavilion which were 2 × 6 mm thick and 2 × 2 m in size with the eight support points.

CHAPTER 6.6

Cold-Bent Glass Panels for Van Gogh Museum, Amsterdam

Fig. 236 Design proposal for the glass wing with entrance at Van Gogh Museum, 2015, architects Kishō Kurokawa and Hans van Heeswijk.

The cold-bent glass façade of the new entrance to the Van Gogh Museum in Amsterdam is a true eyecatcher for any architect and structural engineer. This extension of 2015 was based on a draft design by Kurokawa, who had died in 2007, and then fully developed by architect Hans van Heeswijk [Ref. 26]. Its curve complements the existing stone wing designed by Kishō Kurokawa in 1999 and results in one continuous elliptical building volume. The façade consists of in-situ bent glass units that are connected to the vertical glass façade fins.

When the term cold-bent glass is used, cold refers to the installation process at ambient temperature at which the glass is bent into a certain shape. In industrial production of flat laminated glass units the glass is given a PVB interlayer. Its creep behaviour makes PVB a good choice for cold bending. In reality, laminated glass is always subjected to slight cold-bending due to imperfections in the glass unit itself

Fig. 237 Cross section of the Kurokawa wing (left) with underground connection to the older museum building as designed by Gerrit Rietveld and completed in 1973 (right).

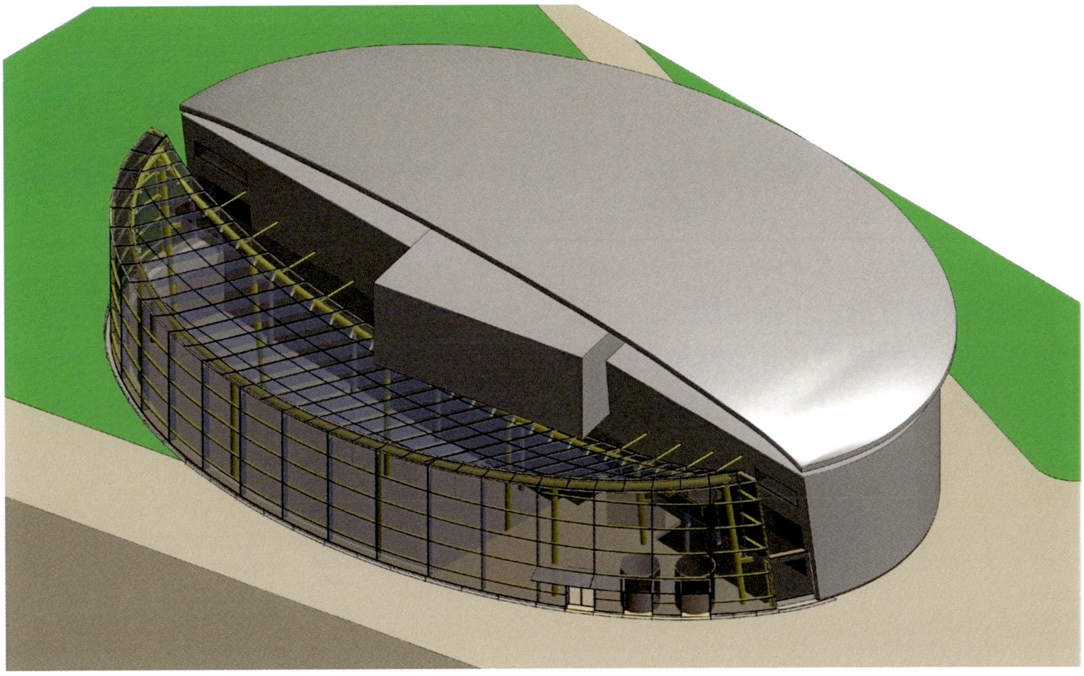

Fig. 238 Isometry of the glass entrance hall of the Van Gogh Museum.

or in its substructure onto which it is fixed. The fixation inevitably induces local cold bending of the glass panels. However, in engineering terms, a façade treatment is called cold-bent when the deformation is more significant and done specifically with a design purpose, after thorough analysis.

GEOMETRY FAÇADE VAN GOGH MUSEUM

At both ends, between the existing stone façade and the new glass entrance, two flat glass panels are placed with a small recess to emphasize the transition between the old and new building. Between these glass units a curved façade of about 60 m in length stretches, with varying height and varying bending radius. The height of the façade is a result of the roof geometry and is varying between 8 and 10 m. The curvature of the façade is directly linked to the elliptical ground plan of Kurokawa. This elliptical shape with varying curvature is approximated by several arcs with a maximum deviation of a few millimetres. The minimal bending radius that results in the highest curvature was found to be 11.5 m. The maximum radius is 42.5 m.

In the first design phase, the centre-to-centre distance of the vertical supporting structure was assumed to be 1.8 m and the height of a glass unit would also be 1.8 m. The façade was facetted. After an investigation of the double curved surface that resulted if one was to bend the 1.8 m glass unit it was concluded that the reflections were undesirable. To get better deflections, a greater width of the glass unit was assumed to obtain more bending length. A length of 3.6 m was chosen, and, after building a mock-up, it was also concluded that the vertical glass fin support in the centre of the glass unit could be omitted. This was quite economical. Thus, a centre-to-centre distance of 3.6 m between the glass fins resulted. In order to achieve an unobstructed view at eye level and to have a rigid element at 1.0 m above the surrounding pavement, the height of the bottom glass unit was set at 0.9 m. The top glass units of the façade all have varying dimensions to ensure a smooth curve with variable height at the top of the extension.

GLASS UNIT AND THEIR SUPPORTS

The cold-bent glass units were connected to glass fins for maximum transparency, which had most likely never been done before. The composition of the glass units consists of a laminated outer and inner pane, both with two sheets of 5 mm heat-strengthened glass and four layers of PVB in between. Normally, two layers of PVB would be applied by the glass supplier to cope with imperfections, but four layers have been opted for due to the lower bending stresses (especially in the long run) as the shear deformation of the PVB reduces shear interaction between the glass sheets. Normally, fully tempered glass is selected in case of cold-bent glass for its higher tensile capacity, but in this case heat-strengthened glass was chosen after detailed analysis, because of their favourable post-failure characteristics. Even when all glass sheets are completely broken, they stay in place.

Fig. 239 Entrance hall

The supports of the cold-bent glass units are custom designed and different from the usual linear clamped edges. The long edges are supported by small screw plates on the outside and a linear element on the inside, while the short edges are supported on the outside by a stainless steel solid linear section and on the inside by a rectangular hollow stainless steel section that is glued to the vertical glass fin. The small steel screw plates at the end of the long edges are used to generate a rotation at the four corners of the glass unit. The screw plates in the centre of the glass unit are structurally active in case of wind suction, which often occurs in a curved building.

Figs. 240, 241 The cold-bent glass façade units of the Van Gogh Museum entrance at night andduring daytime.

The horizontal steel section in between the glass fins is loaded by a bending moment at its ends when the end steel plates are tightened. The steel sections are mechanically connected to the glass fins to be able to partly transfer dead load and wind load. The dead load of the glass panels is transferred by compression from the top panels to the lower panels. This system thus enables the fixation of the glass unit, but due to the stiffness of the glass pane itself, the short edges would bulge if not restrained. In order to have a better reflection these edges are restrained and screwed to the rectangular section that therefore pulls at the structural sealant between it and the glass fin. This is a permanent load acting on the silicone for which the allowable stresses are relatively low. The total thickness of the glass sheets of the fin was needed for maximum tensile resistance. Tape that is applied during the production process as spacer between the stainless steel RHS profile was put at low stressed locations and the application process of the sealant in the factory was monitored closely to make sure this critical detail was executed perfectly [ref 27].

Fig. 242 Testing the specially developed robotic bending machine: after the bending of the insulated glass panel in the factory, simple bolting on the façade can take place.

ROBOTIC BENDING MACHINE

To investigate the bending procedure, fixation, geometry, airtightness, reflections and post-failure behaviour, a mock-up was built in the Octatube laboratory. Two glass units of 3.6 m × 1.8 m and two glass units of 3.6 m × 0.9 m were bent to a frame with a curvature of 11.5 m. First manually, later by using a specially built robotic bending machine. This multi-purpose bending machine was subjected to a test phase. The robot was developed as a combination of a regular glass vacuum lifting machine with two vacuum circuits, and an electrically driven bending mechanism. The bending mechanism was designed to be very easy in use, so one green button was designated for the bending and a red button started reverse bending.

It was calibrated on site to accommodate the different bending radii. Flat IGUs were delivered to the building site first. Then, the bending vacuum machine was fixed onto the glass, the IGU was lifted from the glass stillage and then bent from above to the desired curvature that is measured by the relative deflection. Next, the curved glass in the bending robot was lifted by a crane and hoisted to its destination where the bent form matches the form of the substructure. In order to connect the bent IGU to the substructure, at least the four corner bolts with clamps were tightened and then the bending machine was released.

Opposite page: Fig 243 Result of poststressed and cold bent double glass panels.

CHAPTER 6.7

Hot-Bent 3D Glass Panels

Normally, when an architect designs a curved glass façade or roof, this is executed with hot deformed glass, in laminated panels or in IGUs. These so-called hot-bent laminated glass units are named after the manufacturing process in which the individual glass pane is heated to about 600 degrees Celsius and then shaped (sagged) in a receiving mould. Cooling down can be done naturally to obtain an annealed glass panel or the glass can be cooled instantly by cold air simultaneouslyapplied along both faces of the pane in order to obtain fully tempered glass (very short cooling period) or heat-strengthened glass (longer cooling period). After cooling down, the single bent glass sheets can be laminated by using an autoclave. IGU units of annealed, heat-strengthened or fully tempered glass, can be composed of single or laminated panes, depending on the analysis of stresses expected in the glass and the expected safety behaviour in case of breakage of one of the panes.

Fig. 244 Main building for Santander Group City, Madrid, Kevin Roche, 2004. Fully tempered and hot-bent 3D double glass for a dome of 3 m as per original design in three parts.

Fig. 245 Santander Bank, Madrid. Realized upper glass eye in 3D glass panels, hot deformed in moulds in nine parts.

In the circular roof for the main building of Santander Group City near Madrid, designed by architect Kevin Roche, New Haven, the top had to be filled with an all-glass sphere (diameter 3 m). It consisted of nine identical insulated glass units, all in the shape of a spherical segment and with a smooth curvature also on the edges. The nine spherical components were produced with acceptable deviations from the theoretical model. The glass panels were fully heated and deformed in a jig, and subsequently chemically pre-stressed. The project remained within budget; however, these glass panels proved to be 40 times more expensive than flat double glazing (see chapter 5.4). Usually, it is more economical to use cold bending and twisting of flat glass panels.

In this case the question is for whom do we do this bending with its high costs? And who will notice it?

CHAPTER 6.8
Cylindrical Hot-Bent Glass

Architect Jelle de Jong from Lemmer won a design competition for the covering of the ruins of the Broerekerk, church of Franciscan friars in Bolsward, The Netherlands. The church lost its roof and wooden structure in a fire in 1980. Since then the walls stood bare and unsupported. The town of Bolsward is a little city in Friesland with a picturesque town hall from 1617. The church itself dates from the 13th century. The concept the architect worked out with Octatube Engineering was a steel and glass structure. It has the form of a stepped roof and the interior is a barrel vault. The church previously had a timber roof covered with roof tiles and a timber barrel vault on the inside. The new glass covering for the roof was to be fixed not on the top girders but on the cylindrical barrel-vaulted steel elements. The steel structure trusses would mark the construction while the actual glass roof was suspended. The glass-and-steel construction creates a stark contrast with the masonry walls. And it is this very contrast that makes the design so remarkable.

In the church in Bolsward, the steel structure made of rectangular tubes is quite sleek. The roof structure rests on the cambering walls but is structurally independent from them. The walls, however, are stabilized in horizontal direction by the steel structure. The glass panels in the ceiling were hot-bent panels as they were too curved for cold bending with a radius of 5.8 m. The panels were 1.2 × 1.5 m and they each consisted of two panes of 8 mm heat-strengthened glass, laminated with 1.52 mm PVB. The engineering of the project went fluid, as was the production of the steel elements.

In the church in Bolsward, the steel structure made of rectangular tubes is quite sleek. The roof structure rests on the cambering walls but is structurally independent from them. The walls, however, are stabilized in horizontal direction by the steel structure. The glass panels in the ceiling were hot-bent panels as they were too curved for cold bending with a radius of 5.8 m.

Fig. 246 External view of steel structure and glass roof for Broerekerk, Bolsward, 2006, architect Jelle de Jong.

Fig. 247 Broerekerk, Bolsward. Through the roof steel structure it is hard to see the glazing.

Fig. 248 Interior view of the glass roof for Broerekerk, Bolsward, 2006, architect Jelle de Jong.

The panels were 1.2 × 1.5 m and they each consisted of two panes of 8 mm heat-strengthened glass, laminated with 1.52 mm PVB. The engineering of the project went fluid, as was the production of the steel elements.

However, several cylindrical glass panes broke shortly after installation, were replaced and broke again. More than half of the glass panels broke, exhibiting jumping cracks in a brickwork-like pattern. Most likely, the German producer had not handled the heating and cooling process properly. The glass panels were laid in a fixed mould with steel rods and twisted chord around the rods, so as to have small contact points and much air to blow around during cooling. The points of rope supports were in fact not pre-stressed during the cooling. In order to do that the glass panels had to move in the fixed mould during cooling. As the breaking continued, glass panels were eventually ordered from Sunglass in Italy. These panels had a different safety concept: only the outer panes broke, not the inner ones. So in case of breakage, the panels were kept in place by the inner unbroken pane. Never was a panel destabilized or fell down, testifying to the strength of the lamination concept.

The German producer paid most of the expenses of replacement, sold his machinery equipment and retired from his profession.

CHAPTER 6.9

Curved Glass Building for Spartherm, Melle

The Spartherm project in Germany had two new aspects for Octatube: glass panels to be bent vertically and the German specialty of the individual building permit 'Zulassung im Einzelfall' (specific planning approval). The architects Podufal-Wiehofsky had designed an office building for Spartherm, a company owned by Gerhard Manfred Rokossa, specialized in fire places for homes. The building had the form of an extended ellipse: the roof and side façades were continuously bent glass planes and the two flat front and back façades were conceived as a cable net façade. The building has a flame form as it was to be seen from the highway A3 running from Osnabrück to Hannover. Octatube took the experience from both the cold bending at the Van Gogh Museum and the cable net glass façades of the Rotterdam Markthal into account.

Figs. 249, 250, 251 Spartherm Office Building, Melle, summer 2020, architects Podufal-Wiehofsky. The flame-shaped building (top) and its glass components (bottom).

The design of the building is from 2012. Meanwhile, the architect was no longer involved by the client in the further elaboration and execution of the work. In 2020 the client turned 80 years old. He considers the construction of this building as a recognition of his life's work in the community of Melle.

Fig. 252, 253
Bending of the glass panel with the bending robot in the Octatube factory.

The function of the building is office and showroom, the storey height has to do with the fact that the client wanted the building to be visible from the motorway. When the work began, it was not yet clear what functions the floors would have. When the concrete construction was completed, the building made a strong Corbusian impression. A bit of a shame to cover it with a smooth glass skin?

In 2015, the tests of cold bending the very large glass panels for Spartherm were carried out at the Octatube plant by the 'Institut für Massivbau' of the TU Darmstadt of Prof. Jens Schröder [ref 28]). The size of the panels is 5.5 m height and 2.6 m width. The panels are bent over the long direction. A new bending robot has been developed for bending these large panels. See photo 252. The 4 central pistons adhere vacuum to the glass while the two arms, each with two pistons, pull the glass outwards from the machine until the glass has reached a deflection of 120mm (20 m radius). In this condition, the suction robot with the glass panel is lifted from the ground floor to the position on the roof and is, as it were, screwed on to the 4 corners and in the middle of the long side. The construction photos are not yet attractive because the building is still in its scaffolding and the flame shape is no longer clearly visible, only on the end façades which, incidentally, have been given a simple cladding and lattice facade.

CHAPTER 6.10

Restaurant Nacarat, Hudson's Bay, Amsterdam

Fig. 254 Mock-up of steel structure and cladding component with large and slightly curved glass opening.

At the address Rokin 49 in Amsterdam the existing Hudson's Bay office building was topped up according to the design of architect Kees Rijnboutt in the form of a cylindrical shell structure in RHS sections, clad with a mixture of glass and aluminium panels. These cladding components were all slightly curved according to the curvature of the cylinder which had a radius of10 m. The diagonal subdivision of the space frame was necessary for structural reasons: then all RHS profiles would be loaded more equally compared to vertical semi-circles and horizontal connectors. This diagonal positioning resulted in rhombic cladding components so that the bending of the glass and the aluminium had to be executed at the diagonals of the rhombs. In order to ensure high quality and quick assembly all cladding components were prefabricated in the factory of Octatube, so that only bolting the four corners and sealing the outside would be necessary. The roof panels at the top have only small glass openings, while the components at the bottom have the largest glass panels giving a free view over Amsterdam at the fifth floor level.

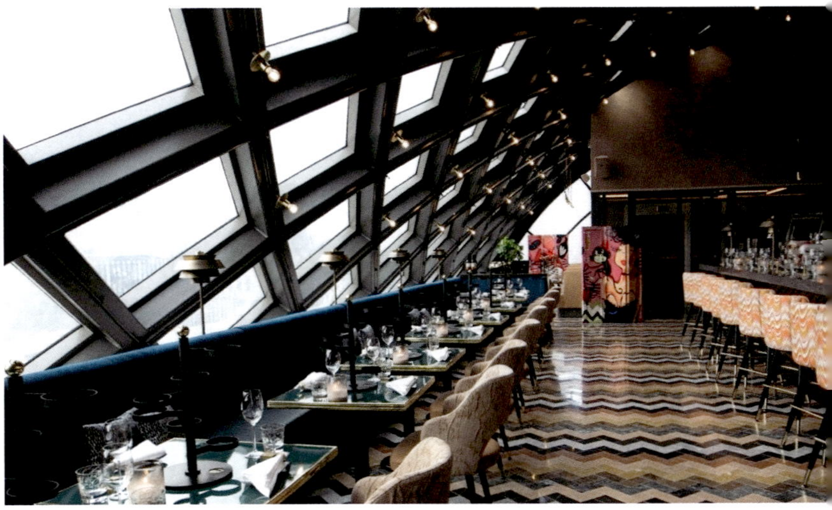

Middle: Fig. 255 Rendering with roof view of the building.
Bottom: Fig. 256 Interior of the Nacarat restaurant with a view over Amsterdam, 2016, architect Kees Rijnboutt.

CHAPTER 6.11

Triple Glazing Eye for Antarctic Research Project

Fig. 257 Isometric view of the red pavilion on skis with the two bull's eyes, 2017, architect Hugh Broughton.

Architect Hugh Broughton designed the new British arctic station Hailey VI, which has been built by the Kaapstad-based contractor's firm of MMS Technology. Octatube was invited to manufacture the two big bull's eye roof lights, with triple glazing in curved glass, fully tempered and with a specialdetailing to allow for the high temperature variations in the arctic climate.

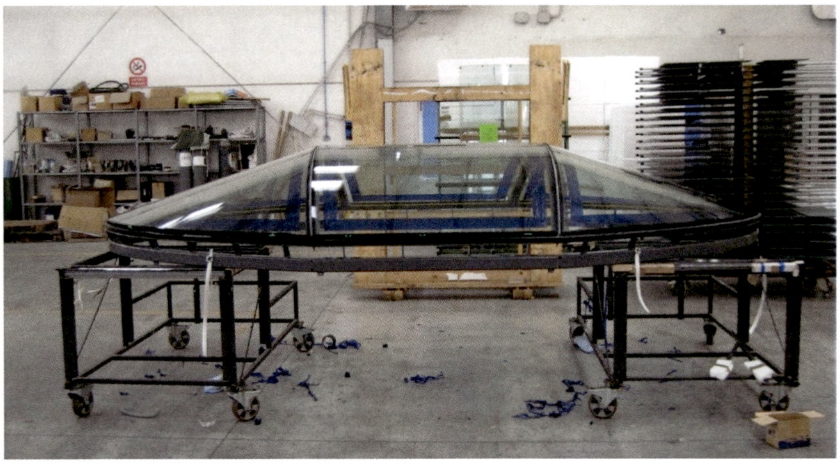

Fig. 258, 259, 260 Detail, mock-up testing and final composition of the entire Hailey project on the south pole. All modules stand on skis to be able to relocate them horizontally, pulled by trucks, or vertically (in case of ice melting). In 2017 the entire project was moved 100 kilometres due to a big rupture in the ice cap.

CHAPTER 6.12

Super yacht, London

For a hotel consortium in London naval architect Tim Saunders designed a floating five-star hotel in the form of a super yacht of 170 m length, in the bestMediterranean design fashion. It started with an idea to make a building without the necessity to buy expensive London ground. This building was to be constructed of world scale low economies and high qualities as a movable building-under construction. The budget price per cubic metre was derived from a skyscraper laid flat. Maritime costs are about four to ten times higher, depending on the degree of luxury. The structure of the ship was to be built on a steel pontoon as a skeleton with steel beams and columns and the hotel rooms were to be completely furnished and prefabricated in Dubai. The cladding was to consist of 2D/ 2.5D aluminium and 3D glass fibre-reinforced polyester (GRP) panels plus flat glazing (2D), bent glazing (2.5D) and some 3D pieces of glazing to be made in the latest state of the art of cold bending and cold twisting by Octatube in Delft. Our experiences in 3D cladding deformation, frameless glass structures and with bent and twisted glass panels would come together in this masterpiece. However, building permission turned out to be much more of an obstacle than anticipated and the project was never realized.

What was interesting was the highly international building process: The ship hull could be built in India or China economically, then towed to Dubai where a legion of 200 Indian carpenters would build the luxurious rooms. After that the ship would be towed to London and moored in the East India Drydock as an example how building can float and be moored as flexible property.

It was later that we understood that the project developers had purchased an existing superyacht which has been moored now I London as the 'Sunborn London Yacht Hotel'. In Gibraltar a similar yacht is functioning as the 'Sunborn Yacht Hotel Gibraltar'.

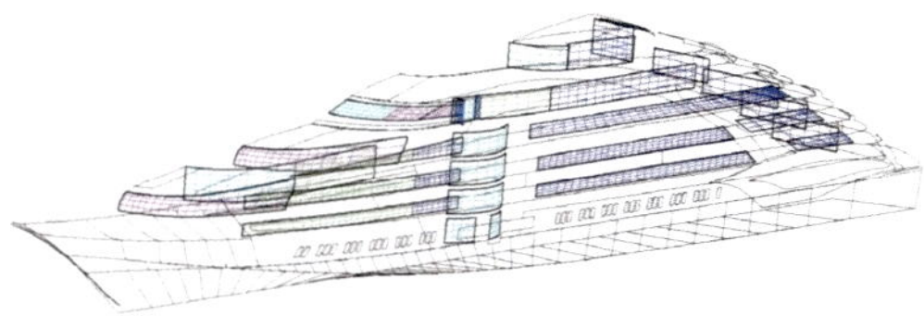

Fig. 261, 262 Proposed super yacht with cold bent glass and aluminium panels. Original ship design by naval architect Tim Saunders. Ferry Ship alternative as a floating building.

CHAPTER 6.13

Glass Greenhouse, Malmö

Fig. 263 Design proposal for landscape architect Monika Gora.

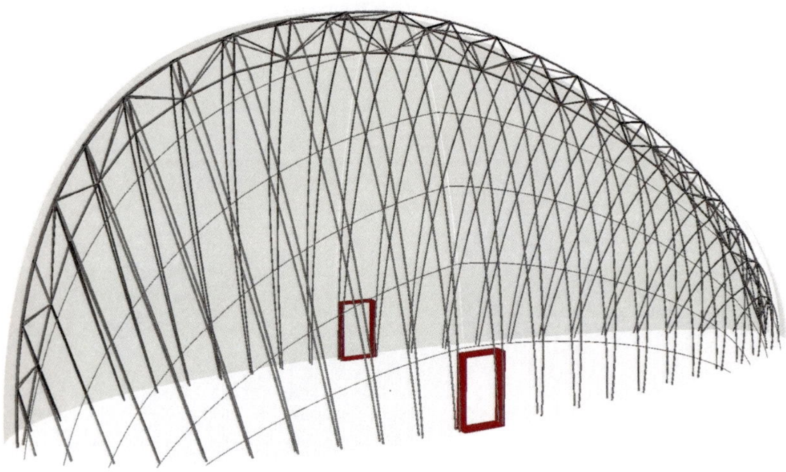

Fig. 264 Geometry of the steel structure with all glass panels positioned without bending or twisting.

Not only the shape of the greenhouse within the Neptuna estate in Malmö is special, the technical aspects of the project are also very interesting. The control of the complex geometry as well as the structural design were very carefully approached to ensure that both were up to the high standard a project like this was asking for. The goal set by landscape architect Monika Gora was to develop a construction with as much transparency as possible. She asked Prof. Ian Liddell of Buro Happold of Bath, UK, to support her design with a structural scheme suitable for tender. A major consideration was the realization of the glass house with flat glass quadrangular panels. This model was tendered for internationally. Some Swedish companies as well as our Dutch company tendered. After comparison of price, quality and experience the project was awarded to the Delft party. Early on in the redesign phase, Monika Gora provided us with a small physical surface model of the greenhouse and a 3D CAD drawing that the glass producer's engineers could work with. As the 3D drawing was not nearly accurate enough to establish a working basis for the further engineering process, a new computer model had to be developed. This was done using sophisticated design software (like Maya and Autodesk Mechanical Desktop). Rendered visualizations helped to finalize the shape.

Early in the design process the decision was made by Buro Happold to use only flat glass panels for the outside surface.

Although the Octatube engineers had ample experience with twisted and bent glass panels the use of hot-bent glass panels was ruled out, as the cost for cladding the complete building with free-formed panels would be too high. Cold twisted panels (panels pressed into shape on site) might have been an option but were also ruled out, as their twisted

surface shape is difficult to control. Cold twisted panels normally form a hyperplane (known from tent constructions), which would have conflicted with the chosen shape of the greenhouse. The challenge therefore was to develop a geometry for the glass panels that would follow the designed shape as closely as possible, while keeping all the glass panels flat. This could have been solved easily by dividing the surface into triangles. This easy solution was abandoned, as triangles would mean many more glass divisions with extra silicone seams and glass nodes, which would have compromised the aspired transparency of the surface. Instead a natural growth algorithm was used to develop a surface consisting of flat panels with four corners, starting at the highest point of the greenhouse and working onwards and downwards to both ends of the building. A number of different divisions of the surface were worked out, adjusting the parameters for the generation of the four corner panels each time to arrive at a solution which had logical divisions and endings at all places. By using the natural growth algorithm it was made sure that all panels were perfectly flat, while every corner point of every panel still remained exactly on the originally chosen surface! The glass panels were each made from two laminated, heat strengthened glass panes, 8 mm thick. In order to achieve a façade as transparent as possible, all

Fig. 265 Neptuna greenhouse, Malmö, 2006, landscape architect Monika Gora. Facade detail of the greenhouse with single glazing.

glass panels were made from a special, extra white (low-iron) glass. Also the glass for the doors and the louvre systems at the bottom were made from extra white glass. This glass material has a very low level of iron, reducing the normal, slightly green tint of the glass to almost zero. A considerable glass thickness was necessary, as the location of the greenhouse is exposed to high wind loads, being situated directly at the boulevard on the seashore of the Öresund between Sweden and Denmark.

For the glass node a special clamped connection in the seam between the glass panels was chosen. This connection consists of stainless steel plates, both inside and outside of the glass, with a plastic spacer in between. Four clamped glass nodes are fixed to one spider with four arms. Each of the spiders was laser-cut from a steel plate and bent into the necessary shape. Due to the complex geometry of the surface none of the spiders is the same. A central bolt to the steel structure inside the greenhouse then fixes the spider. The clamped connection allows the use of the glass surface for stiffening the whole structure, as each glass panel can transmit forces in its plane through the plastic spacer to its neighbour panel. This would have been impossible with a drilled connection due to the high stresses around the holes in the glass. The glass surface is therefore used as a continuous shell.

A very simple and legible structure of a double tubular spine with single tubes as legs was chosen. Along the ridge of the greenhouse (the backbone) a double beam made of CHS profiles with a 168 mm diameter was installed. As columns behind each glass seam, CHS profiles with a diameter of 159 mm were used. Overall this choice results in a clean appearance of the greenhouse and high transparency of the façade. To minimize the steel structure, the glass surface is used as a shell to reduce overall deflections. The joints between the different steel parts are made by sleeve connections, to achieve a continuous appearance of the CHS profiles. All connections of the structure are designed to be moment bearing, to reduce the profile dimensions as much as possible.

For production and assembly the highest accuracy had to be administered. Due to the choice to keep all parts as small as possible almost all adjustment space was left out.

Fig. 266 Detail of the single glazing joining using grey coloured sealant.

The glass panels were fitted into the glass nodes with a tolerance of ±1 mm. This tolerance between the glass and the plastic spacer of the glass nodes was then filled up by silicone strips, as otherwise the glass surface could not work as a shell and reduce deflections of the whole structure. The glass seams between the glass panels were made weatherproof by using structural silicon sealant.

Realizing this greenhouse structure as a free-form design taught the engineers that the virtues of different structural schemes have to be employed and that insight in tubular structures has become ever so complicated. By combining the structural action of shells and space frames and even of structures with bent elements, the greenhouse structure could be made. The engineering required a great many bent tube pieces in very different bending radii. The accuracy of producing structures assembled from bent elements of different radius is well- known. Appearing tolerances and neutralizing them in order to arrive at a structure with a high tolerance, dictated by the use of frameless glazing that cannot allow larger tolerances than 1 to 2 mm at very seam, requires a production and frequent 3D surveying during production and assembly stages. The result, however, shows a great visual logic.

Top: Fig. 267 Night view of the Malmö greenhouse.
Bottom: Fig. 268 Night view of the Malmö greenhouse interior.

CHAPTER 7.
GLASS FINS IN ARCHITECTURE

SAFETY BEHAVIOUR OF LAMINATED GLASS

For years and years, much research on the safety of glass structures has been undertaken and there have been major developments. The safety of glass panels was vastly improved when monolithic glass was substituted by laminated glass. It was generally required that individual glass panels would be strong enough to resist the loads of the workers for overhead glazing and would not shatter under their weight. This is easier to achieve with heat-strengthened glass rather than fully tempered glass. But the principle is that while overhead glass panels may break they nevertheless have to stay in place and must still be able to carry the live load of two men. The safety of glass beams is a completely different matter. If a glass beam was to break and collapse, it would initiate a process of yielding of the glass panels. It is important that a glass beam stays in place and continues to support the glass panels. For glass fins, the same requirement applies: never must a glass fin yield as this would be followed by a progressive collapse of glass panels, which is dangerous and potentially lethal for users of the building. The glass fin has to stay in position under all circumstances, broken or not. The lamination is advised to be a triple lamination, so that both side glass panes could be broken and the middle one would still remain active.

In 2014, a test was done in the Octatube laboratory on the residual strength for that purpose. It marked the end of the material quest for 'Zappi' and has been described more in detail in chapter 7.6. A triple-laminated fully tempered 7 m long glass fin as used for the Municipal Museum in The Hague (see chapter 7.3) was included in a mock-up and subjected to practical loads. Successively all three panels of the laminated fin were deliberately broken and after the breaking of the central panel the fin was sagging slightly, but kept its position for 4 weeks, which proved to be a safe behaviour of this structural component for roofs. See also figure 300 in Chapter 7.6.

Opposite page: Fig. 269 Medieval & Renaissance Galleries at the Victoria & Albert Museum in London,2009, architect Muma Architects and engineer Tim Macfarlane. Glass fins with hidden support details.

LARGE-SCALE GLASS FINS

The possibility to produce larger fins by new tempering ovens and lamination ovens began around 2000 and initiated a number of glass structures with glass fins as the major structural beams. The first generation were single solid glass beams in float glass, and a bit later in fully tempered glass. In façades these fins were quite vulnerable to damages. When fins grew larger they were first made of annealed glass. After the initial investments of Seele and NorthGlass, based in Luoyang, that were to enable the production of larger fins for the Apple Stores, production possibilities grew. The Seele fins are perfectly made, but expensive. The NorthGlass fins require an engineer to supervise the project production in order to assure the proper quality. And there is the question of shipment and transport over a long distance and in four weeks of time from China overseas to Europe. Today, In the meantime glass fins are made with triple laminations since a glass pane can be damaged and become inactive on either side and still the central pane has to remain functional.

Fig. 270 Glass fins in the Ocatube factory.

CHAPTER 7.1

Victoria & Albert Museum, London

The first major project with laminated glass fins of different lengths and angles in the roof were the Medieval & Renaissance Galleries at the Victoria & Albert Museum in London, 2009, by Muma Architects and engineer Tim Macfarlane (fig 269). The striking design seems to have the glass fins cut sharply through the Victorian brick walls. The fins themselves, at a height of 12 m, are almost completely transparent and therefore invisible when looked at from below.

Five years later, the V&A asked us to participate in a project for a new main entrance to the V&A Museum on Exhibition Road, where earlier Daniel Libeskind had made a geometrically complicated entrance building proposal of crumpled paper, which was not appreciated in London. Instead of a maximally complicated geometry the new entrance was designed with maximum abstraction in mind, the other extreme.

Amanda Levete Architects (AL_A) had created an open courtyard with a glazed restaurant, a large day-lit underground exhibition hall and new entrance doors below grade, hence downstairs from street level. The design was quite abstract and all materials also were to appear abstract. The architect conceived this project, handled by Wates Construction as the main contractor, as a design & build contract and did not provide any detail planning. This approach made the development process for the builders very demanding with numerous rounds of redesign. We started out with detail sketches in many versions of which a few were turned into mock-ups.

The effect of the glass skylights was indeed quite abstract, with a mix of stainless steel, partially polished, partially matt pearl blasted. The skylights on top of the underground exhibition hall are both direct glass openings and an elongated rooflight where one looks down from the courtyard and sees red coloured longitudinal boxes, architectural elements in the porcelain-tiled floor. A ventilation system had to be developed to ensure that the high overpressures caused by summer temperature within those skylights could be moderated and would not lead to internal condensation or dust collection.

Fig. 271 V&A Exhibition Road Quarter, London, 2017, architect AL_A. Rooflight with glass fins and polished stainless steel perimeter flashings.

Left: Fig. 272 View from the restaurant at the V&A Museum through the conically curved insulated loadbearing glass panels.

Right: Fig. 273 V&A Exhibition Road Quarter. Courtyard with skylight for the underground exhibition space and the red boxes.

Fig. 274 Indoor view of the steel tensile trusses at the NAi, Rotterdam, with half mechanical, half chemical Quattro connections, 1995,architect Jo Coenen.

CHAPTER 7.2

Extension former Netherlands Architecture Institute,

The lobby of the Netherlands Architecture Institute (NAi) in Rotterdam, architect Jo Coenen, 1995, was built in tension trusses and double glass panels (see chapter 3, fig 99, 105, 106, 107). The 2011 renovation and extension, again designed by the office of Jo Coenen and engineered and realized by the second generation Octatube, substituted the tensile trusses by glass fins. This was a move towards a design of more abstract quality. The well-known name of the NAi with its up to 40 architectural exhibitions per year around the millennium became 'The New Institute'.

The original lobby glazing for the NAi as developed by Jo Coenen and Mick Eekhout in 1995 consisted of tensile trusses and insulated glass panels stacked on each other. The glass panels were connected with half mechanical, half chemical Quattro nodes. The trusses were positioned at a 60 degree angle in plan in order to harmonize with the grid of Jo Coenen. During the renovation, the building entrance was moved, the restaurant was extended and spaces for educational activities were added.
As part of this refurbishment, the tensile trusses and the glass panels were removed (all but one in the lecture room) and a new envelope was installed, consisting of larger glass panels stabilized against wind and external loads by laminated glass fins.

This renovation was realized by a succeeding generation of designers (both in the architecture office of Jo Coenen as well as in Octatube) which is manifest in an altered design approach, moving from technological towards abstract thinking. The older designers miss the technical legibility, the younger designers argue that in the overwhelming amount of information, that the building and its exhibitions represent, abstract and inconspicuous components are a better fit. Personally, I was not enthusiastic about this façade solution. In the café at ground level, artwork was installed to create a cheerful environment.

Fig. 275, 276 In the 2011 extension, the tensile trusses were replaced by glass fins: visually abstract and almost invisible.

CHAPTER 7.3

Municipal Museum, The Hague

Fig. 278 Municipal Museum of The Hague designed by Hendrik Berlage in the 1930s before the atrium covering.

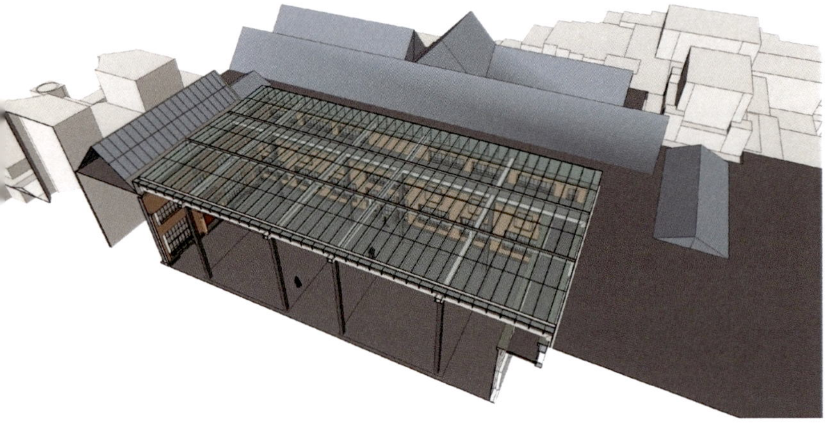

Fig. 279 Isometric view of the proposed flat atrium roof, Job Roos.

In the 20 × 40 m large atrium covering for the Kunstmuseum of The Hague (until 2019 Gemeentemuseum or Municipal Museum), architect Job Roos (Braaksma & Roos architecten), 2014, triple laminated, low iron, whitish glass fins were employed as secondary beams, for the perspective effect of appearing open, when viewed straight from below, and closed when seen tangentially, from the end of the atrium. These fins have a stainless steel connector on top and they are silicone glazed to connect the fin with the insulated, laminated roof panels in low iron glass. In the centre of the atrium, quadruple laminated glass was used for the primary beams, also in low iron glass, spanning 13 m with a structural width of 10 m (in the secondary fins), so the glass fins had to accommodate heavy loads. In the counterlight the main fins in low iron are almost invisible. The roof has been designed to disappear visually, leaving the metal columns and beams as a tribute to the original architect Hendrik Berlage (1856–1934). The side columns

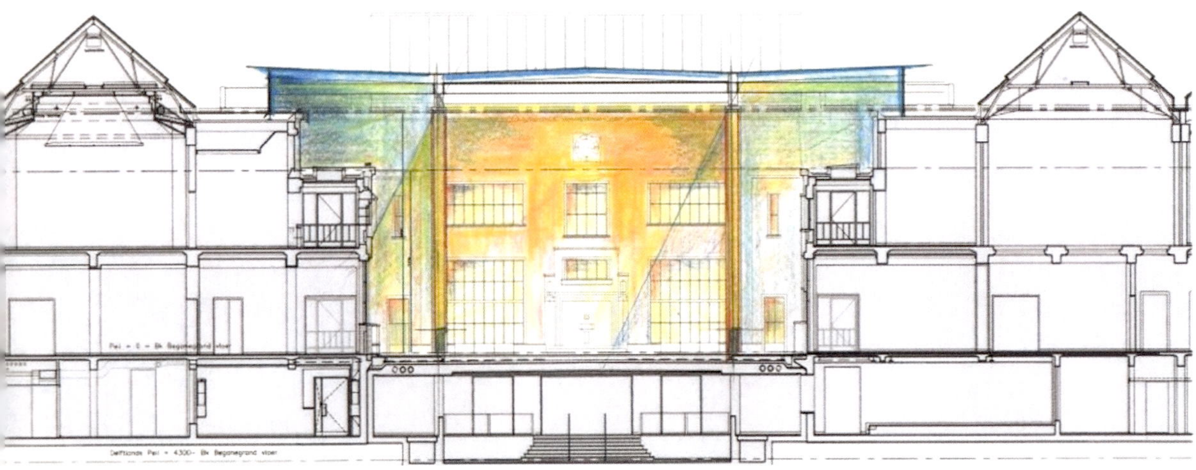

Fig. 280 Section of the atrium covering, drawing by Job Roos.

supporting the outer areas of the roof and the façades are also low iron, triple laminated glass studs of 200 × 30 mm. They make the roof edge fly like an extended wing.

DESIGN

The Municipal Museum in The Hague was designed by Hendrik Berlage in 1931 and opened in 1935. Unfortunately he passed away a year before the opening. Nowadays, the museum is a listed monument. Previously, architect Job Roos had been responsible for a general technical restoration and had added a large basement to the building. Later he received a request from the managing board of the Municipal Museum, Benno Tempel and Hans Buurman, to design a glass covering for the atrium. The atrium of 20 × 40 m was a little used external space with grass lawns, paved paths and an artwork by Sol LeWitt.

The museum increasingly became aware that it lacked a space for receiving larger groups at social occasions, outside of the regular museum visits. Architect Job Roos invited Mick Eekhout as structural designer to participate in the design. While the architect's focus was on Berlage's building, Mick Eekhout contributed his experiences with transparent roof structures as numerous atrium coverings of existing buildings had been realized by Octatube. For example, the Prinsenhof Museum glass hall in Delft of 1997 (see chapter 5.3) was a comparable project since it had a surface of 17 × 25 m and the historic preservation committee required that the glass covering needed to be as transparent as possible. It subsequently became the covered public town square of Delft.

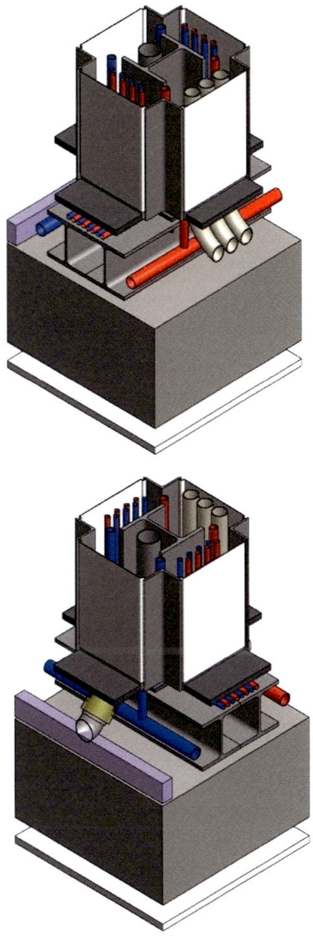

Fig. 281 Detail of column in which piping and wiring for electricity, floor cooling and rain water drainage are concealed.

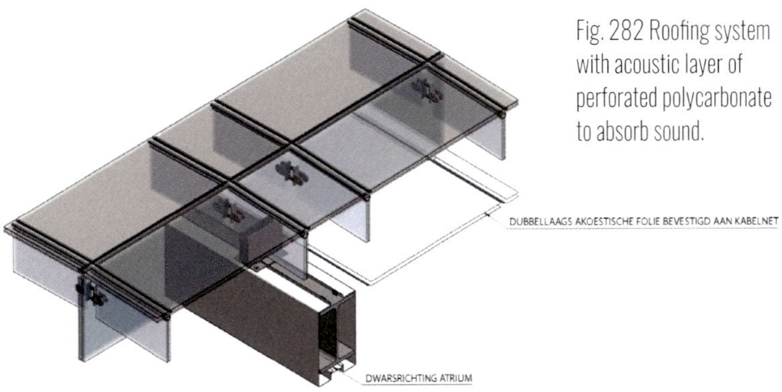

Fig. 282 Roofing system with acoustic layer of perforated polycarbonate to absorb sound.

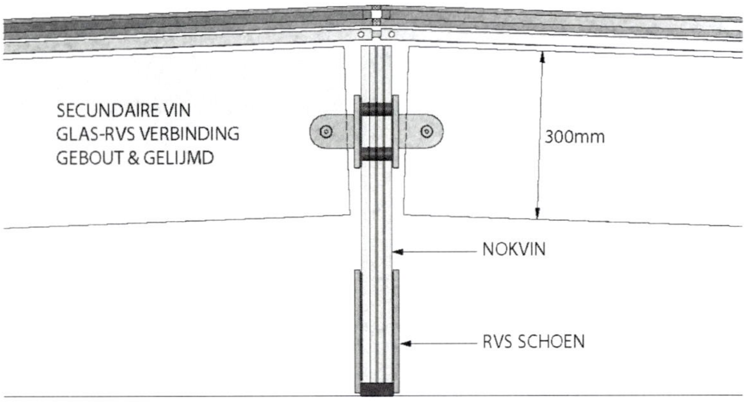

Fig. 283 Connection detail between intersecting glass fins.

Fig. 284 Mock-up of the glass connection, without the top layer of insulated glass panels.

Fig. 285 Interior view of the clad columns and the roofing system with opaque glass fins, creating a play of shadows.

ROOFING AND CLADDING

The dimensions of the insulated glass roof panels are determined by the centre-to-centre distance of the secondary beams, which have a width of 1210 mm and a staggered size of 550 mm at the position of the columns and cross beams. These sizes are derived from the dimensions of Berlage's bricks. Because of the width the glass panels are not extraordinarily thick: the top surface is only 8 mm fully tempered single glass, the lower surface laminated 6.6.2 heat strengthened glass. The top is rigid enough to prevent rainwater puddles from forming. In the length, a span of 7.20 m from the beam to the ridge fin, a single seam of UV-resistant structural silicone sealant was applied. This single seam reduces the risk of leaks and is easy to maintain. The roof panels are 3.60 m long and positioned with an incline of three degrees.

The vertical wall panels with a height of 1200 mm are insulated and laminated glass. Because of the counterlight shining through these panels, they seem to be completely transparent and invisible, as if "they were designed away" as Dutch industrial designer Friso Kramer would say [Ref.17]. In two places glass louvres are provided to naturally ventilate the room if the ventilation system is switched off. At the position of the sloped roof at the rear of the hall, the vertical façade is shortened and is positioned visually on a new gutter in Berlagian materials. This gutter conceals many customized features and details.

GLASS COLOUR

If the roof glazing had been executed in standard float glass, the beams would have seemed greenish due to the thickness and the usual iron content of the glass. This effect was simulated with a mockup skeleton equipped with different types of glass panes and placed outside; light was then projected through the glass upon a white cardboard sheet on the floor. White became greenish – not acceptable for the artwork on display in the atrium. If the famous 'Victory Boogie Woogie' by Piet Mondrian, the museum's most famous painting, ever was to be exhibited in the atrium space, the white in the painting would appear greenish.
Low iron glass or opti-white glass was originally developed to provide the highest possible yield in PV cells. This glass also gives a vastly improved true-colour projection on the floor. This was reason enough for the managing board to have all glass panels and glass fins executed in this type of glass. Due to building physical considerations, a neutral coating was applied on the low iron glass which minimally affects the real visibility of colours, making it acceptable for museum purposes. For the same reason, it was decided to use low iron glass also for the main glass fin and the secondary glass fins. Thus, the glass surface of the main fin seems invisible; the secondary beams appear in a bright white colour instead of whitish with a greenish shade (normal float glass). On a sunny day, the white glass fins also project a graphic shadow upon the Tuscan masonry walls of Berlage.

Fig. 286 Interior view of the glass roof with acoustic ceiling (almost invisible) with a system of LED lights on the cable net. The long central transparent glass beam is heavily loaded by the smaller glass fins.

Next pages: Fig. 287 The glazed atrium of the Municipal Museum of The Hague in use as the central courtyard, 2014, architect Job Roos.

CHAPTER 7.4

Glass Fins for the Van Gogh Museum, Amsterdam

For the Van Gogh Museum extension in Amsterdam, architects Kishō Kurokawa and Hans van Heeswijk, 2015, similar triple laminated glass fins as at the Municipal Museum were employed, but this time completely transparent, in low iron glass, spanning between tubular steel edge profiles that act as the bending/compression elements of the roof. The specific form of the roof required freeform engineering which resulted in complicated shoes welded onto the CHS members to connect the glass fins for the roof and for the façade. The roof fins are covered by laminated insulated flat and warped glass panels. The façades are formed by cold-bent insulated façade panels, forced from their originally flat shape into in a curved form by an electrical robot (see also chapter 6.6).

In collaboration between architect Hans van Heeswijk and Octatube the final design of the new entrance building consisted of a minimal steel structure with a 3D curved CHS tube along the perimeter of the glass volume. This roof beam is supported by ten steel columns. The other main structural elements were all made of glass. The ambition was to provide transparency, visual tranquility and a high level of finish quality. The inverted spheroid surface of the glass roof is supported by 30 parallel glass fins that are all unique in length and height, the longest being 12 m. The steel columns had to be positioned at an angle due to the shape of the glass envelope. The explicit wish of the architects was to minimize the amount of metal components as much as possible.

Fig. 288 Steel structure with glass fins in the roof.

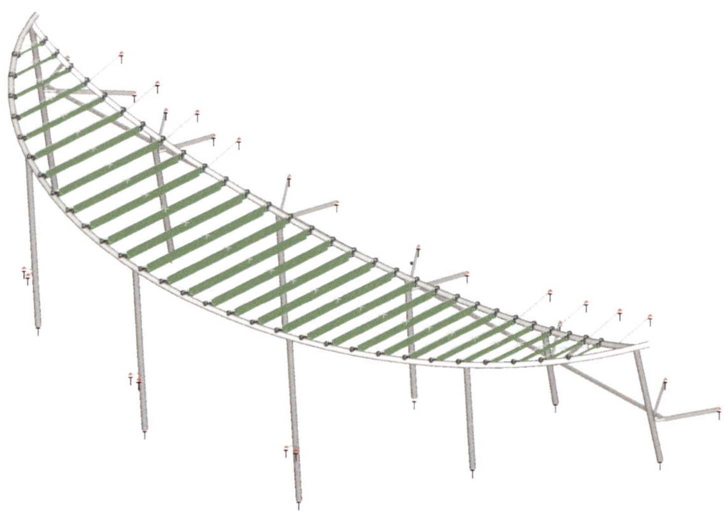

Glass fins therefore acted as beams in the cross direction at every glass panel seam. The glass panel size was 3.6 m horizontally at a height of 1.8 m vertically (the width of the glass panel) to minimize the support structure and visual distortions due to irregular reflections which are very visible when walking by the outside of the façade. Vertical glass fins at every 3.6 m in combination with curved horizontal steel purlins were designed to create a free panorama when looking out horizontally between two rows of purlins. The main structural system consists of two CHS beams on steel columns, connected at various positions and stiffened by the roof glass structure. Thus, steel wind bracings in the façade and the roof could be avoided, the view remained unobstructed and the price level remained reasonable.

SYSTEM DESCRIPTION

The eye-catching elements of the Van Gogh Museum's glass entrance are the façade and roof, both supported by a hybrid system of steel tubes, glass panels and glass fins. The connection between columns and perimeter tubes is rigidly bolted to become a portal frame with hinges at the bottom feet. More stability has been derived from tubular stabilisers to the existing Kurokawa stone wing.
The glass fins are connected to the perimeter tubes to be able to bring over normal forces and to be part of the overall structural system. As glass is usually not used to stiffen steel structures, this method was experimental and hence elaborated on here in more detail.
Normally, both glass fins and regular glass units are mainly loaded by bending forces. Fins are then used to support glazing units in façade and roof structures that primarily absorb wind and snow loads. However, as glass is capable of withstanding high compressive forces, fins can be used as compression elements in a structure. The engineers of Octatube have experimented successfully with glass stabilizations since the mid-1990s. For the Van Gogh Museum extension it was proposed to use the glass fins in the roof to vertically support the IGUs 8/16/1010.4) and to transfer horizontal compressive forces from the curved steel tube next to the façade to the curved beam next to the Kurokawa stone wing.

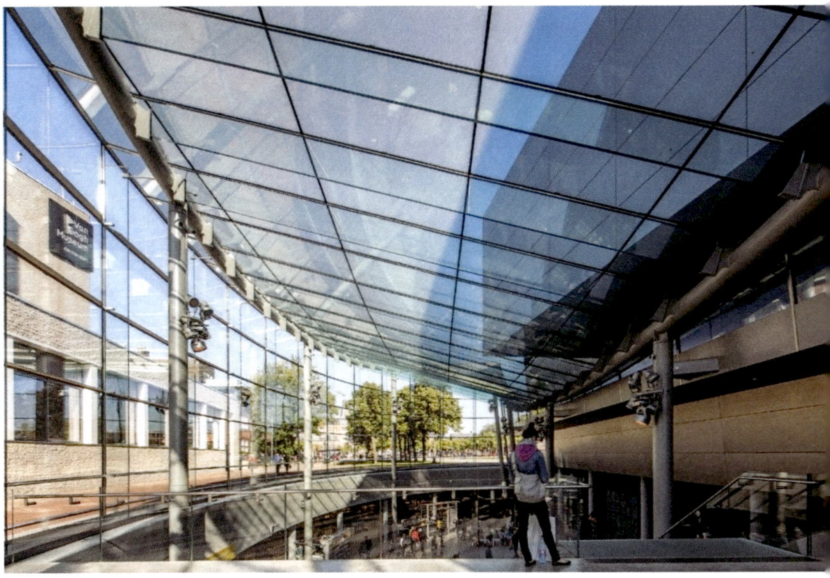

Fig. 289 Interior view of the glass façade and roof supported by a hybrid system of steel tubes, glass panels and glass fins.

Co-authors Chris Noteboom and Jouri Bijster.

To transfer tensile forces, the bonded rectangular stainless steel sections are connected to the steel structure as well. The dimensions of the glass beams are chosen in relation to their span. Due to the elliptical shape of the floor plan and the resulting curved geometry of the façade, all glass fins differ in length. Downward loading, dead load in combination with snow load, is normative for the glass fins. This load is simplified as an equally distributed load on one glass fin. In the design of glass fins, dimensions are governed by strength as allowable stresses are relatively low. A ratio is determined in which this normative (simplified) load combination would lead to stresses equal to about 50 % of the allowable stresses.

Fig. 290 Detail of glass fin–steel tube connection.

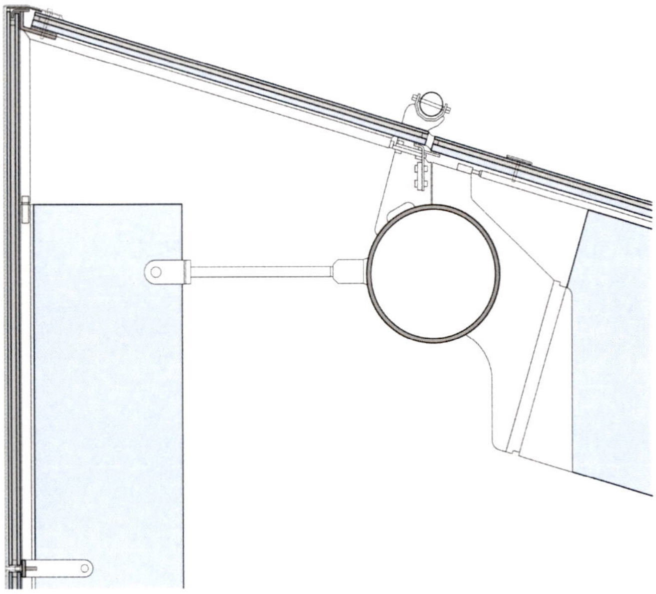

Fig. 291 Detail section of the façade-to-roof connection.
Left: cold bent glass façade panels.
Top: cold twisted glass panels.
Right: flat glass panels.

For the longest fin of 12 m, a height of 700 mm was determined. In relation to the total thickness of less than 50 mm this is a very slender beam and therefore susceptible to lateral torsional buckling. Torsional stiffness of a laminated section is determined by the thickness of single sheets and shear interaction between those sheets. In the analysis the thickness of the interlayer is omitted. Calculations of the glass roof fins were based on the PVB interlayer and showed almost no shear interaction between the glass sheets in case of long-term loading. Therefore, torsional stiffness is mainly determined by the thickness of the single glass sheets. Stability is also determined by lateral support of the beam's surfaces in compression. Stability is increased by connections (centre-tocentre 800 mm) on top of the glass fins to the roof IGUs which have a maximum width of 1.8 m. Thus lateral movement at the top of the glass beam, that is loaded in compression in the normative load case, is prevented. Inverted upward loading due to wind suction is not normative as the dead load of all glass elements is relatively high and the slope of the roof is quite modest. After finite element stability analysis of the glass fins, a glass composition of 3 × 15 mm was determined. A laminate of three sheets was chosen to make sure that after breakage of one glass sheet, the maximum characteristic load can still be resisted by the two remaining panes.

Fully tempered glass was chosen to increase the allowable stresses. In combination with SentryGlas interlayers, the post-failure characteristics have been improved in the event that all three glass panes within a laminated glass roof fin would be broken. However, this is very unlikely as they are high up in the air and cannot be reached by maintenance staff without special equipment. It was found that the normative load case for stresses and stability is snow load in combination with a glass fin that has one broken pane.

Opposite page: Fig. 292 Van Gogh Museum entrance hall. Interior view of the glass roof and minimal steel structure consisting of a 3D-curved CHS tube along the perimeter of the glass volume.

CHAPTER 7.5

Glass Fins in the Elevator Shaft of the Mauritshuis, the Hague

The Mauritshuis museum is housed in a prominent building that used to be a 17th century palace. The Dutch government acquired the building in 1820 to house the Royal Cabinets of Rarities and Paintings and to thus open a royal collection to the public, just like the Louvre. However, due to the increasing interest of the public in art, the shortcomings of the Mauritshuis became apparent. The main entrance was no longer suitable for the growing number of visitors, who had to enter the building through a former service entrance at the side. In addition, the museum was forced to move the permanent collection in order to accommodate temporary exhibitions, depriving the visitors of view of unique paintings that had to be provisionally taken to the depot. The Mauritshuis suffered from its popularity, becoming a victim of its own success (Gordenker 2014), but a solution emerged when a building across the street became vacant. Hans van Heeswijk designed the extension and partly resoration [ref. 29]. The opportunity was seized to excavate the forecourt and the design of an underground entrance foyer connecting the two buildings was born.

Many visitors come to a museum for the first time. Hence a museum's organization can never be too simple and the architecture should be welcoming. In order to satisfy the need for more space and improvement of the public amenities, the underground foyer of the Mauritshuis was designed as a distribution centre. Little is visible at street level except for a cylindrical glass structure which is situated –along with the Mauritshuis itself –right next to the historic Binnenhof (Dutch for inner court) from the 13th century, a complex that houses

Fig. 293 Cross section of the extension for the Mauritshuis, the Hague, architect Hans van Heeswijk, 2014.

Fig 294 Screen shot of the engineering model

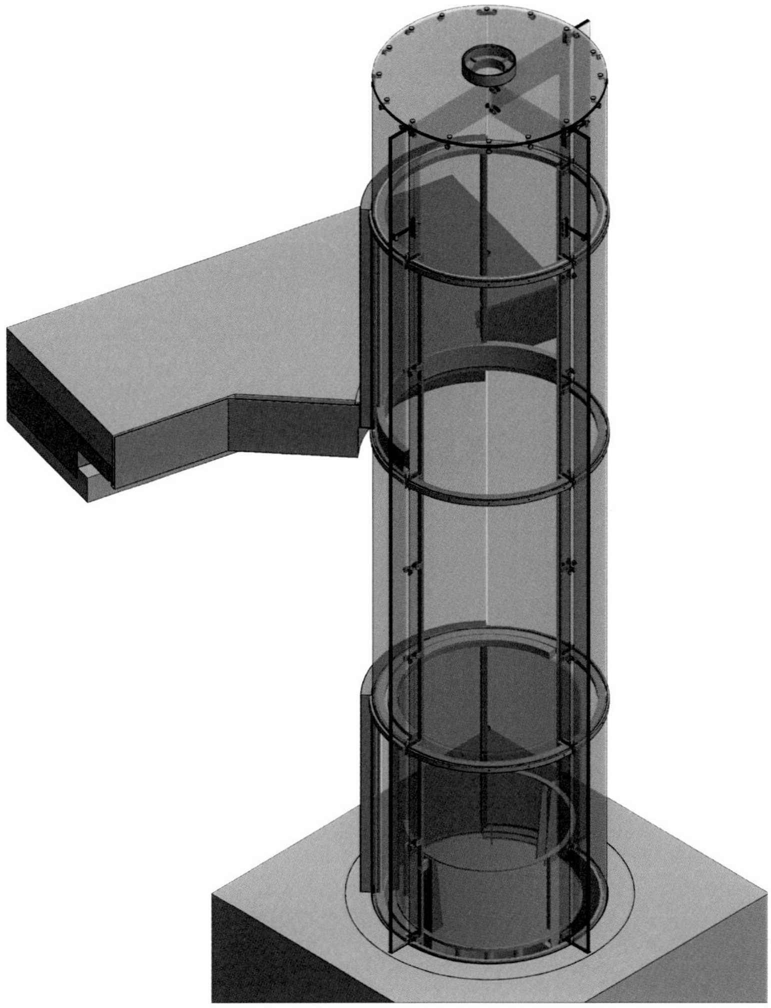

several government institutions of the Netherlands and is one of the oldest parliament buildings in the world still in use. The most prominent structure added as part of the extension is an eye-catching all-glass elevator shaft that also casts light downwards and functions as an urban lantern in the evening. The elevator is an important cylindrical glass landmark that points out the new entrance of the museum and provides a spectacular means to ascent into the museum. The elevator shaft is unique in the history of underground museum architecture because its structural stability is completely warranted by glass components. The principle of an underground entrance has the benefit that visitors immediately have an overview of the layout while they enter from above. The cylindrical glass elevator in the iconic all-glass Apple Cube on Fifth Avenue in New York (by Bohlin et al, 2006), leading to the underground store, proved an inspiration for the glass elevator.

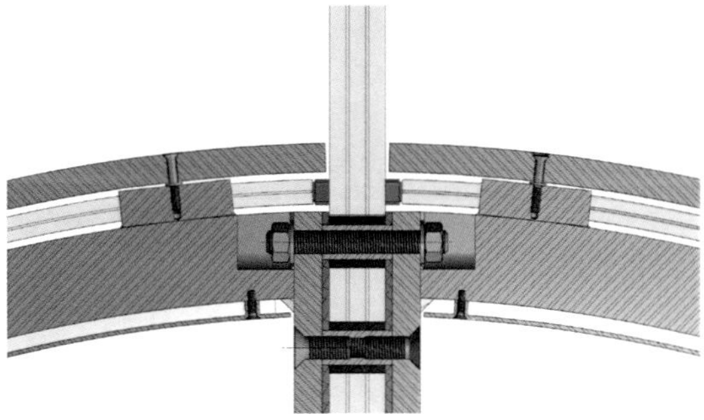

Fig. 295 Horizontal detail section through one of the rings connected to a glass fin.

The total length of the glass elevator shaft is 9 m. The footing of the circular shaft has been rigidly fixed to the bottom of the lower level. Located between the two buildings of the parliament and the Mauritshuis, the shaft has to withstand strong wind forces. The rigidity is provided by the glass fins, cantilevering from the bottom and cross connected at the roof level. Additional stability is achieved by the laminated glass shaft panels, made of two laminated, fully tempered glass panels.

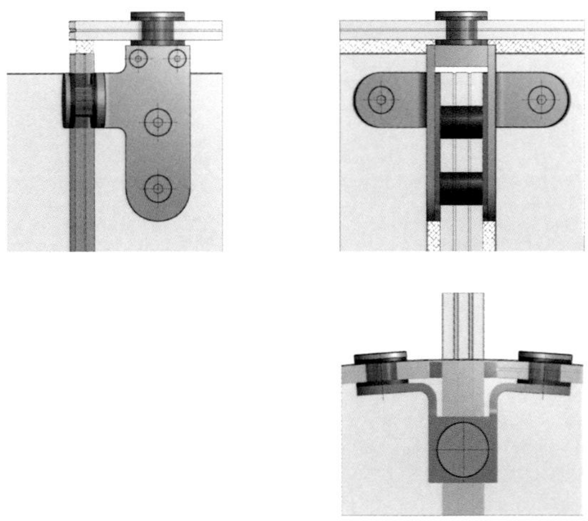

Fig. 296 Roof top edge detail with glass fin connection in section, seen from below and from above.

Fig. 297 Exterior view of the glass elevator from street level. Visitors can walk down on the stairs or use the glass lift.

The connections between the curved glass panels consist of horizontal hoop rings. The laminated circular top glass panel on the roof stabilizes the shaft against horizontal deformations by means of eight corner connections.

The glass elevator embodied two experimental steps: the realization of a cylindrical glass shaft in an outdoor environment with strong wind loads and secondly the employment of two glass fins to guide the sides of the glass elevator cage directly. The original plan to use the fins directly as the guiding profiles for the elevator cage was aborted by the producer of the elevator machinery because of the larger than certified tolerances in the lateral T-profiles that usually guide the cage. At the end a miniscule stainless steel T-profile (50 mm) was chosen as the top guiding profile. Positioning tolerances for this T-profile were agreed upon between Octatube and the elevator producer at the extremely small value of 0.5 mm only. It was the smallest tolerance we ever had to meet. The glass shaft was realized with only a minimum of connecting steel elements. With additional sidelights and a glass floor at the forecourt, the spacious underground tunnel became a well-lit foyer, with the 9 m high glass elevator shaft at centre stage. The Mauritshuis has become twice as large, but its distinctive and intimate atmosphere has been preserved.

Fig. 298 Inside and upwards view of the glass elevator.

Fig. 299 The glass elevator of the Mauritshuis by night at basement level.

CHAPTER 7.6

Where do we go from here?

This chapter is written to close off the material quest for 'Zappi', as an unbreakable non-brittle , yieldable transparent structural material. The compositions in triple layered laminated glass fins appeared to be trustworthy and safe, not in the primary material, but in the composition of glass products such as laminated glass fins, in use as overhead beams of glass roofs.

The younger generation of Octatube engineers uses laminated glass fins as beams in roof structures. Safety is an important safety issue in overhead glazing. Important question would be: What is the residual strength of a completely broken glass fin? For that purpose a test was done in the Octatube laboratory.

Fig. 300 Testing the glass fins at the Octatube laboratory. The fully loaded triple laminated glass fin was fully broken and kept in place (without collapse) for 4 weeks.

A triple laminated fully tempered 7 m long glass fin as used for the Gemeentemuseum / Municipal Museum in The Hague was set up in a mock up with loadings equivalent to the dead weights of the roof plane (glass panels on to of the fin) plus live loading on the roof of a glass fin spaced @ 2m distance. The upper detail contained the stainless steel RHS profile, fully sealed with silicone on top of the fin, on which the glass panels would be placed with rubber of silicone and the occasional clamp to prevent uplift.

The first glass pane of the beam was broken, no deformation. The second one was broken, also without any deformation. Because of the fully tempered character breaking occurred in the usual small fragments of around 10 mm3, held together by the PVB film. After that the middle pane was deliberately broken en gradually a small deformation sag was introduced over the length of the glass fin. This fully loaded and deformed situation without yielding remained for 4 weeks. Normally this time is long enough to attach a brace and / or to replace the broken fin. A brace would be a lower steel profile, triangulated diagonals upward and connections sideward through the upper stainless steel RHS profile between glass fin and roof panel (2014). This test was the conclusion of the material quest for Zappi as a structural glass component material. Would all 'Zappi'-like research & development and innovations stop? Certainly not. In fact 'Zappi' is eternal, but the directions are changed.

What is the lesson from 25 years of the quest for 'Zappi', the hypothetical ultimate structural material? The quest for Zappi is eternal. Zappi stands for an improbable ambition, something that each designer should strive for.

While the quest for Zappi as announced in 1992 did not result in a tangible development on the material level, the research contributed numerous findings in the realm of structural design and details. A number of experimental projects with incremental innovations has yielded safer glass structures for overhead glazing, both in glass planes as in the use of glass beams and glass fins. Loading tests in the Octatube laboratory have resulted in more reliable glass fin constructions.

The more research, developments and designs exist, the clearer it becomes that we never know enough. Glass as a material is not very promising for new adventures. Glass breaks when you do not want it to break, and it does not when it is supposed to break. It is not a very popular engineering material. It lacks ductility and does not emit a warning during overstressing, breaking suddenly. But in the product development world the glass quest goes on. Architects continue to challenge the building industry for the realization of their dreams. The value of developing something new is not a thing apart. Real satisfaction in this development work comes from those victories that are won by the skin of your teeth. When practicing architects dare to design projects without comprehending the technical issues involved in realization, an intriguing challenge may ensue. Both in university research as well as in the company of Octatube incremental steps forwards were achieved to close the gap that architects deliberately had left open between Free-Form Design and Free-Form Technology.

The practice projects of Octatube, however, always went beyond specific architectural designs. In the last 30 years, technical frontiers have been deliberately pushed. As it is the case with university research, it is important to publish the results of these innovative processes.

As each publication, this book is both an end and a new beginning. It is for the next generation only a beginning and wants to pass the torch to the many daring architects working on design experiments worldwide. The more bridges over the gap between architecture and technology are shown, the more new gaps will be created by architects. It is up to technical designers to keep up the pace.

During the two decades of developing a new glass technology in Delft, respect for the material glass and its position in the building industry as a untrustworthy material became very apparent. When building with glass, high investments are required both in terms of effort and in energy. Glass as a material is very costly to make. But it is the main transparent material for architecture. Glass functions as the transparency maker in architecture. Ever since the famous Friedrichstrasse competition design of Ludwig Mies van der Rohe in Berlin (1919), glass stands for transparency in buildings and, by extension, transparency of organizations. With hindsight, Mies would have been happy that he did not win the design competition because at that time they did not have sufficient quality resources (materials, systems) to produce a good building. It would also not have survived the war and would have had to be reconstructed. Now the design has been an ambition for more than 100 years and it was only in the 1980s that it was understood and overlooked. But the symbolism of glass in architecture is clear. There are still many adventures ahead for such a material.

However, transparency is an architectural image and not necessarily a reality. But the symbolism of glass in architecture is persistent. Surely for such a material many adventures lie ahead of us!

Would it be reachable for the next generation of glass industry as a whole to reduce the embedded energy of the entire process from the production of the rough material glass up to the installation of glass facades in buildings and beyond, also maintenance to 50%? 'Zappi' is dead, long live 'Zappi'.

Fig. 301 Scheme of the diffferent phases of the glass production and lifecycle of the facade.

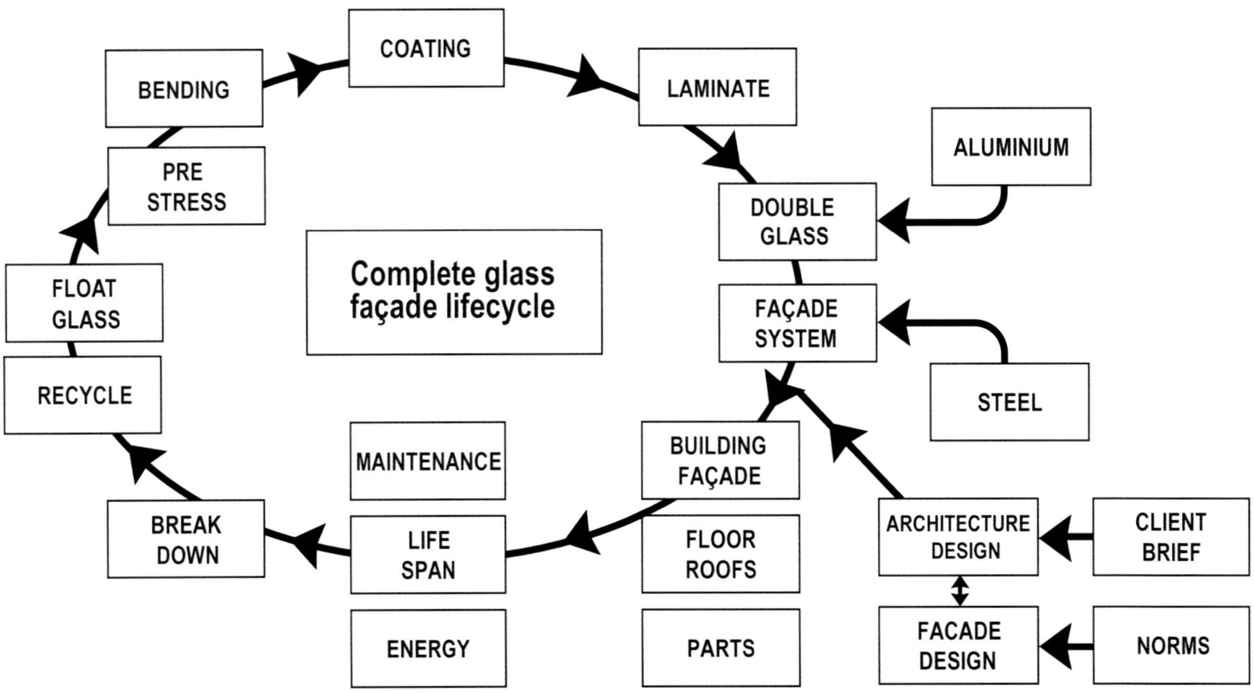

This book documents the many adventures that happened during the quest for Zappi by Mick Eekhout, his team, colleagues of Octatube and some of his students. The PhD students at the Chair of Product Development at TU Delft have the same drive to discover and chart a new territory that was never described before. They were free in the choice of their subjects as long as they believed in it, researched the new and found new insights. In the future, these PhD studies will have to be financed externally, most probably from a SME consortium and EU money, which will give the research much more of an applied character. The Chair of Product Development is situated on the crossing point between the world of scientific research and the industrial world, so no worry there. The PhD students have always enjoyed the frequent exchange between the glass construction industry and the university. And for the more basic scientific work the Dutch research foundations such as the national Dutch research council NWO (Nederlandse Organisatie voor Wetenschappelijk Onderzoek) have to be addressed.

In the company of Octatube a younger generation under the lead of Mick's son Nils-Jan Eekhout is taking over the projects and new initiatives. He is building a more autonomous team of 'Octatubbies' than ever before. The team is very important even though the team leaders will point the way and be persistent in their leadership and innovativeness. The entire team is responsible for the results and enjoys the fruits of their efforts over the years.

This book documents a personal glass footprint. It is about the joy of several decades of professional adventures and innovations. They sometimes were quite risky, even too risky, to be honest, but always worthwhile. Today, one can only feel happy, proud and grateful, thinking of the collaborators in the team, the stimulus from clients and project architects to undertake a new adventure. This book is also about their work and efforts.

Perhaps the best motivation for any continuous quest for innovations results from curiousness, creativity, persistence, a bit of naivety, a positive spirit and belief in ambitions and, of course, the joy in making things that last.

CURRICULUM VITAE
Mick Eekhout

Mick Eekhout (1950) studied architecture at the TU Delft 1968-1973. He worked at the Institut für Leichte Flächentragwerke [IL] in Stuttgart in 1970 with Prof. Dr. Frei Otto and then in the office of Renzo Piano in Genova. Graduated twice (cum laude) on a complex building (Prof. Carel Weeber) and a space frame system (Prof. Jaap Oosterhoff) in 1973. He worked for two years in the architectural offices of Groosman and of Van Kranendonk and started his own architectural office in 1975. In 1983 he founded his design & build company for lightweight structures, Octatube Space Structures. The company designs, produces and builds tensioned membranes, shell structures, space structures, glass structures, frameless glazed facades and roofs, cardboard structures, exploded free-form elements in aluminum, fiberglass reinforced polyester shell structures and tensegrity structures. Incremental innovations are pursued through all structural developments. Today, the group of Octatube companies are involved in projects all over the world with a commitment of 120 fte of people on more than 1000 projects with his son Nils-Jan Eekhout.

In 1989, he successfully completed his dissertation on his own experimental designs: 'Architecture in Space Structures' (cum laude) under the supervision of Prof. Oosterhoff and Prof. Moshe Zwarts.

He was appointed full professor of Product Development in the Faculty of Architecture at TU Delft in 1991.

Fig. 302 Mick Eekhout

The focus of the chair was on design, development and research of high-tech components. From his part-time appointment, he analyzed some of his innovative projects with his students. In education, he started the hands-on Prototype Laboratory. More than 1500 students built their prototypes in this Prototype Lab. Research was done on glass as a material and on freeform technology. As a professor, he built with 40 companies the energy-positive Concept House in Heijplaat, Rotterdam, which unfortunately was demolished by the TU after 5 years, while there was an adequate purchase offer for a second life. Away sustainability! He developed an energy-positive apartment building Concept Urban Villa with a tower in Delft of 16 floors: the 'Black Lady'. He wrote more than 20 books and more than 400 articles.

He organized two conferences on technical design: 'Delft Science in Design'

Fig. 303 Queen Máxima receives the first copy of this glass book at the office of Octatube in Delft during her visit on 17 November 2017.

with many of his fellow professors from all faculties at TU Delft. Standing with one foot in the construction industry and the other in academia, he worked out a master plan for Dutch university research for the construction industry, published in 2009 under the title "Bridging the Gap. In 2003, he was appointed as a member of the Royal Netherlands Academy of Arts and Sciences (KNAW) where he served for three years as secretary of the section Technical Sciences. Since 2003, he has also been a member of the Academy of Engineering (AcTI).
From 2012 he has been focused on the preservation of De Kuip, Feyenoord's famous soccer stadium built in 1937, as secretary of the Reddekuip Foundation. He organized more than eight KNAW mini-symposia in the field of architecture and smart cities. He retired as an active professor in 2015 and continued to work on national research and development for the Dutch construction industry.
In 2017, he turned his focus to the strengthening of earthquake-resistant housing in Groningen. He founded the designer associations Delft Design (1987) and Booosting (1988). In his spare time he loves sailing, enjoying the rigging of the mast and rigging and the cutting pattern of the sails. He enjoys writing, columns and articles in newspapers and for international conferences, books and in the future maybe an adventure novel comparing the Free Form polyester Wings of the Rabin Center in Tel Aviv with the realisation of the Dome of Florence.

This adventurous life would not have been possible without the energy, belief, cleverness and ingenuity of the Octatube engineers and of the entire team that has surrounded Mick Eekhout in all of the described endeavours and many (undescribed) more. Former Dutch State Architect (rijksbouwmeester) Tjeerd Dijkstra complimented Mick in December 2016: "I do not understand that you never suffered a collapse". Thanks to the engineers of Octatube all projects matured from the initial wild ideas to reliable and sometimes certified building systems, functioning mostly as prominent parts in the buildings of satisfied architects and clients. Without the openness of the Octatube engineers to innovation this portfolio would not have been possible.

Fig. 304 The complete crew of Octatube during the visit of her Majesty Queen Máxima and the State Secretary of Economic Affairs,. Mona Keijzer, on 17 November 2017.

REFERENCES

1. Eekhout, Mick. 'Frei Otto and the Munich Olympic Games', Zodiac nr 21, 1972;
2. Eekhout, Mick ed. 'Free Form technology form Delft', IOS PRESS, Amsterdam, ISBN 987-1-61499-553-1, 2016;
3. Eekhout, Mick, Wichers, Sieb. 'Lord of the Wings, The Making of Free form Architecture', IOS Press, Amsterdam, ISBN 978-1-61499-549-4, 2016;
4. Eekhout, Mick. 'Methodology for Product Development in Architecture', IOS Press, Amsterdam, ISBN 978-1-58603-965-3, 2008;
5. Eekhout, Mick. 'Bridging the Gap, 2010
6. Eekhout, Mick ed. '3TU Bouw Leerstoelenboek, 2010;
7. Eekhout, Mick, Van Swieten, Peter. 'Delft Prototype Laboratory', IOS Press, Amsterdam, ISBN 978-1-61499-545-6, 2016;
8. Eekhout, Mick ed. 'Delft Science in Design', TU Delft, Faculty of Architecture, ISBN 90-5269-327-7, 2005;
9. Eekhout, Mick, Tomiyama, Tetsuo, eds, 'Delft Science in Design 2, IOS Press , Amsterdam, ISBN 978-1058603-739-0, 2007;
10. Eekhout, Mick. 'Componentontwerpen en Productontwikkelen', IOS Press, Amsterdam, ISBN 978-90-5199-538-1, 2016;
11. Wittgenstein, Ludwig, 'Tractatus Logico Philosophicus', Wenen, 1923;
12. Eekhout, Mick, 'Emeritaatsrede', TU Delft, ISBN 978-94-90694-03-8, 2015;
13. Eekhout, Mick. 'Architectuur tussen traditie en technologie', Publicatiebureau Bouwkunde TU Delft, ISBN 90-5269-113-4, 1992;
14. Eekhout, Mick. 'Reconstructie en ontwikkeling van het Maison d'Artiste Prototype', Stichting Maison d'Artiste Prototype, Delft, ISBN 978-94-90674-10-6, 2017;
15. Eekhout, Mick. 'Product Development in Glass Structures', Uitgeverij 010, Rotterdam, ISBN 90-6450-111-4, 1990;
16. Eekhout, Mick. 'Architecture in Space Structures', Uitgeverij 010, Rotterdam, ISBN 90-6450-080-0, 1989;
17. Bullhorst, Reiner, Rudolphine Eggink, 'Friso Kramer, industrieel ontwerper', ISBN 978-90-6450-1241, 1991;
18. Wurm, Jan. 'Glasstragwerke', dissertatie Birkhäuser, Basel, ISBN: 978-3-7643-7608-6, 2007;
19. Nijsse, Rob. 'Glass in Structures, Elements, Concepts Designs', Birkhäuser, Basel, ISBN 987-654321, 2003;
20. Wachsmann, Konrad. 'Wendepunkt im Bauen', Vg. der Kunst, Dresden, ISBN: 978-3364001166, 1989;
21. Eekhout, Mick. "Stressed Glass, Zappi or Product Development for the NA'i / , NAi Publishers, Rotterdam 1996, (88 pags) ISBN 90 72469 78 X

22. Womack, James P., Daniel T. Jones, and Daniel Roos. 'The Machine That Changed the World' Free Press, New York, 1990, ISBN: 978-0-7432-9979-4.
23. Sabbagh, Karl. 'The making of a Skyskraper' Viking, New York, ISBN-13: 978-014-015-284-5, 1990;
24. Vollers, Karel. 'Twist and build, creating non-otrthogonal Architecture', NAI Rotterdam 2001, ISBN 978-90-G450-410-5
25. Staaks, Dries, Eekhout, Mick. 'Cold Twisting of Glass', Octatube International bv Delft, 2012;
26. Van Heeswijk, Hans, Kloos, Maarten. 'Van Gogh Museum, Het Gebouw, nai010 uitgevers, Amsterdam, ISBN: 978-94-6208-262-5, 2015.
27. Bijster, Joeri, Eekhout, Mick, Noteboom, Chris 'Glass Entrance for Van Gogh Museum' artikel over Van Gogh, Challenging Glass Conference, Springer, 2011.
28. Schneider, Jens, 'Versuchsbericht: Experimentelle Untersuchung der Stoß- und Resttragfähigkeit an zu Reinigungs- und Wartungszwecken betretbaren Verglasungen' , Institut für Werkstoffe un Mechanik, Darmstadt, Nr. 102.01.14, 2014.
29. Quentin Buvelot, Jaap Huisman, Hans van Mierwijk, 'The Mauritshuis', 010 Uitgevers, ISBN 978-94-6208-145-2
30. Ebbert, Thiemo, 'Reface, Refurbishmnent Strategies for the Technical Improvements of Office Facades', TU Delft, ISBN 978-90-8570-499-7, 2010;
31. Schröder, Hans, De Wit, Ruud. 'Bloedstollend vastgoedverhaal Markthal Rotterdam: van idee tot icoon', JGMS Holding B.V., ISBN-13: 978-908-278-100-7, 2017.

FOTOGRAPHERS / IMAGES

Alice de Groot: Fig. 285
ASFotografie.nl: Fig. 173, 174
Dario Scagliola: Fig. 147, 131
Hufton + Crow Photography: Fig. 273
Interpane: Fig. 22, 110, 111, 185, 187, 188
Jacqueline Knudsen: Fig. 298
Luuk Kramer: Fig. 229, 239, 240, 289, 290, 297
Michael van Oosten: Fig. 292
Ossip van Duivenbode: Fig. 31, 204, 207, 209
Paul van Gaalen: Fig. 91, 92
Ronald Tilleman: Fig. 241
Robin Utrecht: Fig. 303
Wiebe Kiestra: Fig. 304
Fig. 97: www.theimaginativeconservative.org/2016/03/sword-of-damocles-no-friends-tyrant.html
Fig. 164: www.glazenzaal.nl

CREDITS

'GLASS DESIGN INNOVATIONS IN ARCHITECTURE'

Texts: Mick Eekhout
Corrections: Ria Stein, Berlin
Editor: Mick Eekhout
Lay out: Nicole Harmann, Germaine ter Brugge
Design Cover: Studio Maud van Rossum

Thanks: to the teams of Octatube for designing, engineering, production and assembly / installation and to members of the Chair of Product development TU Delft

Printer: Printerpro, Rotterdam
Publisher: Octatube, Rotterdamseweg 200, 2628 AS Delft, The Netherlands
info@octatube.nl / sales@octatube.nl / www.octatube.nl 00.31-15.789.0000

The book is published as the completion of structural design activities by Mick Eekhout as the pioneer, director and main structural designer of Octatube is nearing. His son Nils-Jan eekhout is currently managing director of Octatube. The retirement lecture at the TU Delft was done in 2015.

Distribution: nai010 publishers, Korte Hoogstraat 31, 3011 GK Rotterdam
info@nai010.com, sales@nai010.com

nai010 publishers is an internationally orientated publisher specialized in developing, producing and distributing books in the fields of architecture, urbanism, art and design.

nai010 books are available internationally at selected bookstores and from the following distribution partners: North, Central and South America - Artbook | D.A.P., New York, USA, dap@dapinc.com www.nai010.com

ISBN 978-94-6208-6722

2022 2nd issue Octatube